Praise for *Better Together*

"When it comes to gender issues in the workplace, ministries, and life in general, it's pretty obvious we're facing significant challenges. Thankfully, Danielle Strickland has written this timely, needed, and necessary book, *Better Together*. Danielle has a unique ability to navigate tricky terrain with truth, boldness, gentleness, and courage. This book will not only lovingly correct, but also inspire and instruct both men and women with grace and understanding. We need each other to do everything we are called and created to do! This subject is important to God. As Danielle writes, 'We aren't just cleaning up a mess. We are building a new world.' And we are unquestionably better together!"

—CRAIG GROESCHEL, PASTOR OF LIFE.CHURCH AND
NEW YORK TIMES BESTSELLING AUTHOR

"In *Better Together*, Danielle Strickland provides a practical and timely picture of what could be. A glimpse of the 'strategically hopeful.' Freedom fighters, justice advocates, influencers, and thought leaders all united to not just dream of a better story, but to actually create one. Grab this book and join the movement!"

—BRAD LOMENICK, FOUNDER OF BLINC AND AUTHOR
OF *H3 LEADERSHIP* AND *THE CATALYST LEADER*

"This book should be required reading for every Christian. Drawing on years of experience, research, and with great grace, wisdom, and prophetic insight, Danielle urges us to pursue healthy relationships between men and women, for the sake of our witness in this world, to fulfill the mission of the church and for future generations."

—CHRISTINE CAINE, FOUNDER OF PROPEL WOMEN AND A21

"I consider Danielle Strickland to be a world-impacting leader and that just about anything she says ought to be taken very seriously. *Better Together* is such a book. It is a compelling call to restore the God-given co-agency to women in every domain of society. It's been two thousand years since Jesus set women free from oppressive patriarchy—let's get this done already!"

—ALAN HIRSCH, AWARD-WINNING AUTHOR OF *REFRAMATION* AND 5Q, FOUNDER OF MOVEMENT LEADERS COLLECTIVE, FORGE INTERNATIONAL, AND 100 MOVEMENTS

"It's hard to think of a subject more universally important than this, or a person better positioned to address it than Danielle Strickland. At a time of such pain and antipathy between the sexes, Danielle's voice rings out with prophetic conviction and biblical clarity, mapping out a path for reconciliation and hope."

—PETE GREIG, 24–7 PRAYER INTERNATIONAL AND EMMAUS RD, UK

"Danielle Strickland understands what it means to fight for a better future. She realizes brokenness leads to better stories and difficult conversations lead to better connections. In this book she addresses the inequities and injustices that make it nearly impossible, but even more important to have a level playing field. Whether it's recognizing opportunities to improve or acknowledging obstacles that keep us from being better, Danielle has unusual and compassionate insight. This book doesn't offer easy answers or casual blame. Instead, Danielle insists that we drive toward solutions that celebrate both our differences and our diversities. For Danielle, it's not political; it's personal. It's personal because of the people she's known, the realities she's seen, and the overpowering hope she holds to."

—REGGIE JOINER, FOUNDER OF ORANGE/THE RETHINK GROUP

"Danielle Strickland is perhaps one of the greatest minds in Christianity today. Anything she writes is guaranteed to change your life or the way you view God."

—SAM COLLIER, INTERNATIONAL SPEAKER, TV, AND RADIO HOST OF *A GREATER STORY*

"There are more than a few gaps remaining in the relationship between men and women in leadership. Danielle does a brilliant job of compelling us, men and women alike, to work toward a strong, healthy future. What you lose in ignoring the issues costs everyone, including you. If you're looking for practical steps to take and compelling reasons to take them, this book holds the road map."

—CAREY NIEUWHOF, AUTHOR AND FOUNDING
PASTOR OF CONNEXUS CHURCH

"There is an urgent need for the message Danielle is presenting in her latest book, *Better Together*. The church greatly needs this reminder to rediscover the Edenic vision of male and female co-reigning in mutual honor and interdependence (Genesis 1:26)—thereby bringing the kingdom of God to earth."

—COLONEL JANET MUNN, DIRECTOR OF THE SALVATION
ARMY'S INTERNATIONAL SOCIAL JUSTICE COMMISSION

"Danielle Strickland is not only a world-class speaker who can inspire a room of thousands; she is a passionate activist for justice and compassion. Spending time with Danielle inspires you that mercy is worth pursuing and change is possible. That is illustrated in this book on equity, a subject that is crucial for our world to grapple with right now. Read this and be ready to play your part in the revolution."

—DR. KRISH KANDIAH, SOCIAL ENTREPRENEUR,
CONSULTANT, AND AUTHOR OF *FAITHEISM*

"Danielle Strickland is one of the most important prophetic voices of our time. In her new book, *Better Together*, she brilliantly outlines the current cultural divide between the sexes and then, with visionary inspiration, shows us the way to a better tomorrow. This is a must-read book!"

—DAVE FERGUSON, AUTHOR OF *HERO MAKER*

"When the church restricts the voices of women, we are all impoverished. Christians need to learn equally from both aspects of the image of God—male and female—and that means we have a lot of catching up to do. I am convinced that the world needs this book now more than ever. *Better Together* provides us with a vision of what the world could be if men and women really lived as if the kngdom is now."

—BRUXY CAVEY, SENIOR PASTOR AT THE MEETING HOUSE, AUTHOR OF THE END OF RELIGION AND (RE)UNION

"Danielle Strickland leads the way in addressing a vitally important issue for the church. This book is fascinating, challenging, and timely. It is well-researched and beautifully written by someone who is a role model in the area of unity and reconciliation. I recommend it highly."

—NICKY GUMBEL, VICAR OF HOLY TRINITY BROMPTON CHURCH, FOUNDER OF ALPHA, AND AUTHOR OF THE BIBLE IN ONE YEAR

"This is an incredibly important book! We desperately need to create a better world, and Danielle Strickland unpacks how to do it—together. I recommend this book for every person trying to live a better way."

—JO SAXTON, DIRECTOR OF 3DM AND AUTHOR OF REAL GOD, REAL LIFE

Better Together

Better Together

HOW WOMEN *and* MEN CAN HEAL *the* DIVIDE *and* WORK TOGETHER *to* TRANSFORM *the* FUTURE

Danielle Strickland

W PUBLISHING GROUP

AN IMPRINT OF THOMAS NELSON

Published in Nashville, Tennessee, by W Publishing, an imprint of Thomas Nelson.

Published in association with The Bindery Agency, www.TheBinderyAgency.com.

Thomas Nelson titles may be purchased in bulk for educational, business, fundraising, or sales promotional use. For information, please e-mail SpecialMarkets@ ThomasNelson.com.

Scripture quotations are taken from the Holy Bible, New International Version, NIV. Copyright © 1973, 1978, 1984, 2011 by Biblica, Inc. Used by permission of Zondervan. All rights reserved worldwide. www.Zondervan.com. The "NIV" and "New International Version" are trademarks registered in the United States Patent and Trademark Office by Biblica, Inc.

Any Internet addresses, phone numbers, or company or product information printed in this book are offered as a resource and are not intended in any way to be or to imply an endorsement by Thomas Nelson, nor does Thomas Nelson vouch for the existence, content, or services of these sites, phone numbers, companies, or products beyond the life of this book.

ISBN 978-0-7852-3014-4 (eBook)

Library of Congress Control Number: 2019946338

ISBN 978-0-7852-3015-1

Printed in the United States of America

20 21 22 23 24 LSC 10 9 8 7 6 5 4 3 2 1

To Stephen Court. We are better together.

Contents

Foreword by Bob Goff   xiii

The Map   xvii

PART 1: WHERE WE ARE GOING

Chapter 1: Starting from the Future   3
Chapter 2: What It Could Look Like and Why It Matters   11
Chapter 3: The Truth About Oppression   27
Chapter 4: A Vision for Reconciliation   39

PART 2: WHERE WE FIND OURSELVES

Chapter 5: How We Feel: The Pull Back of Fear, the Push
       Forward of Action   51
Chapter 6: How We Live: The Pull Back of Segregation,
       the Push Forward of Proximity   67
Chapter 7: How We See: The Pull Back of Patriarchy,
       the Push Forward of Clarity   79
Chapter 8: How We Think: The Pull Back of Rooted Beliefs,
       the Push Forward of Transformed Beliefs   89

CONTENTS

Chapter 9: How We Connect: The Pull Back of Porn,
      the Push Forward of Truth   99
Chapter 10: How We Act: The Pull Back of Power Abused,
      the Push Forward of Mutuality   111

PART 3: HOW WE GET THERE

Chapter 11: Stopping the Blame Game   133
Chapter 12: Start Now and with You   149
Chapter 13: Never, Ever Give Up   163
Chapter 14: Keeping Hope Alive   175

Acknowledgments   189

Notes   193

About the Author   203

Foreword

contentment ≠ comfort, or lack of discomfort

I try to live by a simple rule: <u>love everybody</u>, always. It may sound easy, but I've learned that simple is far from easy. For love to be realized in real life, it requires us to <u>take risks</u>, <u>tell the truth</u>, <u>embrace discomfort</u>, <u>press through difficulties</u>, <u>change our minds and our behaviors</u>, and most importantly, <u>engage in relationships with each other</u>. Our best learning is done in an environment marked by <u>equal parts truth and kindness</u>.

The truth often makes us uncomfortable. We can see this in the increasingly difficult discussions surrounding the relationships between women and men these days. You've heard the reports gushing out of the movements arising out of cultures of abuse and harassment. You've no doubt read the statistics that one in three women will experience sexual abuse in her lifetime. These are horrific numbers. Many women around the world can't walk home after work without legitimate fear of being attacked. Many women can't raise their voices, at all, for fear of reprisal. In many countries girls can't go to school. To put it simply—this is not okay. Something needs to change. We need to speak up with kindness and unbending resolve about the truth of these things. We need to listen to the truest voices, not just the loudest ones. The reason is simple: you don't need volume when you're right.

In this book you're going to hear from one of the truest voices in my life. I am Danielle's student in many areas and have been for years. She has burned down more than a few of my beliefs to expose the truth behind them. Here's the thing. It didn't feel like she was an arsonist when she did; she sounded like a wise friend.

Men are also in a challenging loop. The statistics feel condemning, and some of the more truth-filled voices have turned harsh and resentful. Every motive, it seems, is open to being publicly questioned, and every action put under a microscope. It seems as if this has left many male leaders afraid. And fear never leads to anything good. Simply put, something needs to change.

But here's the good news: the solutions might not be as daunting as we may think. That's what I love about Danielle—she tells the truth but laces it with hope.

In *Better Together*, Danielle doesn't sugarcoat the painful and embarrassing truth—that's not what love does. She also doesn't make the mistake of oversimplifying the problems. Attacking the complexity of the issue with appropriate rigor, she presents insights, research, and actionable solutions to change things now in order to transform the future for our kids and their kids.

Whether we're opening a Love Does school for girls in Afghanistan or Mogadishu, Somalia, creating a safe house for young women in Uganda, or celebrating the news of becoming a grandparent myself, I know that we all possess the power to change things for the next generation. Even more than that, I know that confronting injustice and inequality and looking for ways to create a better future are what love looks like. Love without action isn't love; it's merely an idea, and we've heard all the ideas. What we need are examples. Danielle is one of them, and I'm with her. I'm willing to take a look at the ways inequality works so I can change it. I'm willing to acknowledge that the relationship between men and women is in some places broken so I can do my part to fix it. I'm willing to embrace uncomfortable and hard things now so the future can be different for my grandkids. And if you can relate to this willingness to learn, then this book will help you.

Better Together is not a woman's book. It's not a declaration of war nor a plea for peace. It's a book for anyone who is courageous enough to realize they, like me, have much to learn. Let's do this together. We can dream about creating a better world, reconciling the genders, and living without fear, or we can wake up and start doing it right now. Let love, kindness, and truth be our greatest tools in the effort.

I hope you will read this book with an open mind, an open heart, and an open hand. I know that if you do, you will learn to love from one of love's wisest teachers. And a life rooted in love, with a hand open to receive, is what it will take to move us toward what you might only have imagined to be a distant possibility. That might be what I like the best about this book and its author—Danielle makes distant possibility seem like a no-brainer for today. She lives and breathes in the currency of what could be. She sees the problem but also the possibilities. And this might be what we need more than ever before. Men and women were made to work together to transform the future. Not separate work, but together work. It is not only a winning formula for change; it's a way of love that is the most transformational currency on the planet.

Buckle up. Here's to a conversation about reconciliation, vision, partnerships, hope, equality, mutuality, and freedom. Once we read about it, while turning these pages in private, let's join together in living out what love looks like in public.

—Bob Goff, Chief Balloon Inflator and bestselling
author of *Love Does* and *Everybody, Always*

The Map

For any journey it's helpful to have a map. Maps offer perspective, but they also help us plan the trip. The graphic on the following page is an attempt to show you what I've envisioned as a map of the mental process from where we are right now in our current relationship crisis, to where we want to be (reconciled, restored, and thriving as we live and work together in peace) and how we get there.

Our journey toward a transformed world where women and men can work better together will require us to start from the future. As you know, that's the beauty of a map. It helps us see where we want to go, our future destination, and figure out how to get there.

When it comes to social change, we don't usually think of the future or of maps. So though it may be counterintuitive, it is essential that we determine just that—where we want to end up so that we can figure out how to get there.

The Transformed Future

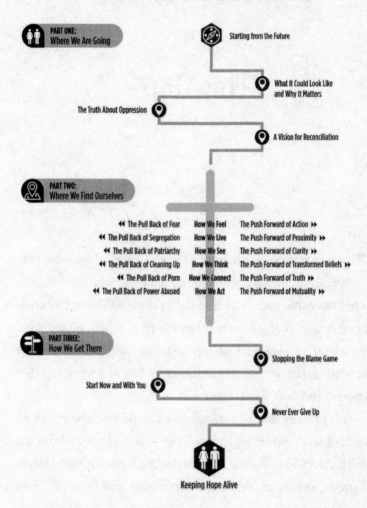

PART ONE:
Where We Are Going

Starting from the Future

What It Could Look Like
and Why It Matters

The Truth About Oppression

A Vision for Reconciliation

PART TWO:
Where We Find Ourselves

◀◀ The Pull Back of Fear	How We Feel	The Push Forward of Action ▶▶
◀◀ The Pull Back of Segregation	How We Live	The Push Forward of Proximity ▶▶
◀◀ The Pull Back of Patriarchy	How We See	The Push Forward of Clarity ▶▶
◀◀ The Pull Back of Cleaning Up	How We Think	The Push Forward of Transformed Beliefs ▶▶
◀◀ The Pull Back of Porn	How We Connect	The Push Forward of Truth ▶▶
◀◀ The Pull Back of Power Abused	How We Act	The Push Forward of Mutuality ▶▶

PART THREE:
How We Get There

Stopping the Blame Game

Start Now and With You

Never Ever Give Up

Keeping Hope Alive

Think of it this way: **We aren't just cleaning up a mess. We are building a new world.** A world where we can embrace our differences, end oppression, and learn how to live and work together in harmony, prosperity, and peace.

It occurred to me while I was mapping out this journey that everything we do right now is either a pull back from or a push toward a transformed future. There is no neutral ground. At the center of the map is a cross because, in all honesty, Jesus is the only sure way to get from here to there. He is the only hope we have for restoration.

As we position ourselves at the cross, we will find we have the strength to push toward the future of a better world. If not, we will easily pull back even more into our present hopeless, deteriorating condition.

Each of us faces this invitation personally, but I sincerely hope we hear it collectively. I have a hunch it'll be a helpful exercise to explore the push and pull of our current opportunity toward restored relationships. Like a workout regimen, there will be things to pay attention to, proper posturing, pacing, and new exercises that will get us in much better shape if we are intentional in our pursuit. I'd like to make some real progress. So be prepared for practical and applicable content. And don't be afraid to give it a try.

But here's the deal. There is no magic bullet or fairy godmother who will fix this problem. It is up to us. We will shape the future by what we do or don't do right now. Are we willing to do the work required to change the trajectory of history? Are we willing to acknowledge where we are and where we want to go, and do we have the courage to take the steps necessary to move forward? These are questions that each of us and every community will need to answer for ourselves.

This is a strategic time for that answer to be a resounding yes! I'm praying that as we catch a vision of a different future, we will have the audacious faith and tenacious actions to live it out, together.

PART ONE

Where We Are Going

ONE

Starting from the Future

Real change comes when people are enabled to
use their thinking and their energy in a new way,
using a different system of thought, different language, and having fresh visions of the future.

—SCILLA ELWORTHY

had read several dozen Twitter comments and I was tired of it.
Yes, I had agreed to speak at a conference recently rocked by
accusations of sexual misconduct and harassment by the founder.
The tweets kept accusing me of kowtowing to patriarchy. *How
could I speak on a stage built by misogyny?* they asked. They said
it was obvious that I must not care about the voice of abused
women. I must admit, I do a fair job at ignoring dumb comments
by misinformed people on social media, but these seemed to be
low blows.

Friends started to connect, and the conversations began: Was I ignoring my responsibility as a woman? Was I missing an opportunity to stick it to "the man" (not just one man but structures and systems that have benefited from ignoring the blatant and dangerous realities of patriarchy for centuries)? Was I benefiting at the expense of victims? As I talked it out and thought it through, I began to realize just how difficult this time is for all of us.

I've longed for equality to emerge as a realistic and rational way to live in our world. I've yearned for mutual thriving. I've experienced men and women working together, and I've been enriched by it. I've read of the impact women's empowerment has for the whole global community. And I remain completely convinced through the Scriptures that true mutuality is the original sacred design of humanity.[1] Men and women are meant to work together for the flourishing of the world. When you spread that idea, people seem to agree. Mutual flourishing? Yes, please. Thriving together? Absolutely. And yet our world remains divided and dismissive of the gender equity dream. I think the real dilemma is not in the *what* but the *how*. *How* do we do it?

In this era people are paralyzed. I realized if my decision to simply speak at a leadership conference was filled with such difficulty, how much more difficult would it be to live out the principles of equity and empowerment for both women and men in everyday life? How can a man interact with a female colleague without his relationship becoming either robotic or flirtatious? How can we work together without suspicion or fear at a time of heightened suspicion and fear? How can we change and challenge systems without taking a side? Who is the enemy, anyway?

Women who demand change? Men who abuse them? Silence and fear? Systems and structures? *I mean, who do we blame?*

This can be confusing. I've worked for decades with women who have suffered at the hands of men. And I mean *suffered.* I remember driving home one day after hearing the story of one particular woman I was working with who was tortured (yes, literally) in an extremely horrific way for a long time and by many men. It was infuriating. I wondered, after hearing yet another story from a woman who had been so humiliated and abused at the hands of even more men, if there were any good men in the world. *Is it even possible for men to be good to women?* I really wondered, on the brink of despair.

But right as those thoughts began to sink into my heart, I pulled into my driveway. My four-year-old boy met me at the door. He had a huge smile on his beautiful little face, and he wrapped his arms around my heavyhearted body and gave me a great big four-year-old bear hug. I could feel my despair lifting. That night, as I tucked him in bed, I went through our regular nighttime ritual. "Who made you?" I asked my little boy as we cuddled under his fire-truck blankets.

"God made me!" he replied with a big, beautiful smile.

"How did he make you?" I asked him.

"He made me good," came the rhythmic reply. And when I looked at this little grinning guy, something shifted in the depths of my own being. I knew it was true. And past the doubt, fear, cynicism, and despair, beckoning me to pay attention was a piece of gold buried in a pile of life experience. When I dug deep down into the truest of truths, I agreed. God made him good.

Trying to stuff down the reality of my day, but without success, I wondered if the goodness of this moment was destined to be lost. Does my little boy even have a chance of growing up good in a world where women suffer at the hands of men in such a predominant way? Plan International states, "Globally, it's estimated that 1 in 3 women will experience physical or sexual abuse in their lifetime."[2] One in three.

Now, to be sure, abuse happens to everyone—boys and men are also abused. At least one in six men have been sexually abused or assaulted as children or as adults.[3] Those rates of abuse are not good. But the disturbing truth is that even when boys and men are abused, their abusers are male: "According to a 2010 National Intimate Partner and Sexual Violence Survey, 90 percent of perpetrators of sexual violence against women are men. Moreover, when men are victims of sexual assault (an estimated one in 71 men, and one in six boys), 93 percent reported their abuser was a man. It's true that women also assault men, but even when victims of all genders are combined, men perpetrate 78 percent of reported assaults."[4]

So I'm aware of all those stats and I'm looking at my four-year-old boy and I'm wondering if he is somehow destined for "badness." And then I snap out of it. Of course he isn't destined for "badness." Of course what happens to men is not fate. Men don't become abusers by accident. Women don't become abused by God's design. We aren't trapped in some fatalistic setup. We aren't animals who can't seem to choose between our instincts and our behaviors. We aren't robots who can program ourselves out of our humanity. We are human. *We can choose.* We can change. We

6

can grow and learn. We can become different and better. If the trajectory of human history has taught us anything at all, it's that change is possible! You can almost hear the scriptural invitation from God almighty: "I put before you life or death. Choose life" (Deuteronomy 30:19, my paraphrase). It is precisely because we can choose that we can change.

We can choose another way to live together. This choice is collective and personal. We choose together, but we also make the choice for ourselves. I can choose another way. Another way for my son and for everyone else's sons as well. I can refuse the shackles of fatalism that repeat the patterns of previous generations. I can choose to refuse to believe that my son, because he was born male, is someone predestined to become part of a patriarchal system of oppression toward women. I can be part of that choice by helping him discover that his behavior can contribute to the making of a better world. I can raise him to appreciate and value women. He can learn to work with them in a respectful and mutually flourishing way. He can be good—indeed, even more than that, he was designed for goodness. I know him better than anyone else on the planet. He is not marked or set or stuck in some distorted destiny to be an abuser or a dismisser or a harasser or a jerk. He was made to be good. And to be good includes learning how to work with everyone, especially women, to make the whole world good again. Which is the work of the gospel.

If ever there was an example of a good man, it is the person of Jesus. The perfect man. He did not live to be an exception to the rest of humanity. He died and lived to change the possibilities for humanity so everyone could join him in being good. This is why we call it good news. It's a restoration movement that seeks to move everyone toward transformation. Including the relationships between women and men.

That's why I'm writing this book. I refuse to believe that all men are bad. I also refuse to believe that all women are victims. I don't want to just be hopeful, I want to be *strategically* hopeful. I want to strive toward a better world where women and men can work together and not against each other.

I was on a pilgrimage with the movement Amplify Peace recently. Part of our journey was to spend some time learning from Sami Awad, a nonviolence activist from Bethlehem. Sami has been using his life to make peace in a region of the world that is extremely divided. The hostility is high. The divisions seem embedded in history. Change is hard to fathom.

Sami spoke to us about the frustration of trying to help people who have suffered from long-term systemic oppression. When he looked into previous campaigns for change, he found that people often tended to dig into their past to discover strength to gain momentum for the future. They typically tried to reach back for something from their origin story to help them overcome their present story. But the trouble with that method for Sami and his Middle Eastern friends was that the more they tried to dig into their past, the more oppression they found. He didn't know how to overcome the reality of a linear momentum theory.

One day he met someone who showed him a different strategy. He was fascinated to discover a theory called nonlinear theology. To put it very simply, it's the idea of starting from the future. You use the potential of the future to get your momentum for change. Instead of digging through the past, trying to sort through every injustice and oppression—like a magician pulling a never-ending ribbon out of a can, or a knot that only becomes more knotted as you try to untangle it—you leave the past in the past for a moment and start fresh with a smooth, clear future.

So Sami hosts multifaith vision sessions where Jewish, Muslim, and Christian widows come together. They spend some time envisioning their future. They picture themselves at the end of their lives, in their rocking chairs on the porch of their houses. Then they share what they envisioned. And here is where the transformation begins. They discover that although they all come from such difficult and different backgrounds, they share the dream of a better future. All of the widows envision similar things. They see their children and grandchildren playing in peace. They picture everyone they love with enough, sharing and loving each other. They see the people they love alive and happy, belonging and contributing to the goodness of the world. They envision peace. And in a small amount of time, in that little, simple exercise, they realize that their dreams for the future are the same. Suddenly they have found some common ground. Some shared hope. Some way of mobilizing their efforts in the same direction!

I think the systemic oppression at the heart of the relationship between women and men is as complex as it gets. There is an old joke about a genie who is summoned and tells the master who called him that she can have only one wish. The master wishes for peace in the Middle East. The genie begs her for a simpler task, complaining about the impossibility of the wish. So the master says she's been looking for the perfect man who would make for a perfect relationship. The genie says, "Fine. Peace in the Middle East it is!" To be sure, if we were to try to undo the knot of gender relationships, it would feel impossible. But I think the strategy Sami uses might be a more effective one for change.

When I dream of my son's future, I'm deeply aware that my dreams are much like the ones you have for your sons and daughters. Whether you have a girl or a boy, or you're thinking of your brother or sister, husband or wife, mother or father, your dreams for them are the same as mine. I dream of a peace-filled life. I dream of flourishing and thriving. I dream of happiness and hope. I dream of meaning and purpose. I dream of fulfilled destiny and celebrated gifts. For my children, I dream of them contributing to the redemption of this world.

If we pay attention, I think we will discover that our dreams for the future are the perfect starting place for changing our present. We have much more in common as we reach into our shared future. Rather than just rehashing the problems of the past, we can move forward together. Honestly, if we were to try to wade through the intricate brokenness of the relationship between women and men, we would need a much bigger book! Instead, let's take a strategy out of Sami's playbook and start with the future. I'm believing that our shared view of our future world looks like equality, freedom, and flourishing. This is the future we are all hoping for.

TWO

What It Could Look Like and Why It Matters

At the heart of humanity's present evolutionary challenge is the need to heal and transform the relationship between women and men. Not only does this relationship affect all the other social, political, and economic realities of our world, it influences the larger relationship of humanity with the Earth, with the larger whole of life. It is a crucible for the entire drama.

—RICHARD TARNAS, PHD

remember when my son went to his first day of kindergarten. We were living in Australia at the time, so it kind of felt extra special and especially scary. I thought about him all throughout the day and couldn't wait until I picked him up so that I could hear all about it. It went something like this:

"Zion, so how was your first day of kindergarten? Was it just awesome?"

He responded the way he has responded to many other school days since: "It was boring."

I was shocked. How could it have been boring? It was Australia and it was kindergarten! He explained that all they did the entire day was tell stories about what they had done over the summer break. I asked him what he had shared.

"Well, I wanted mine to be really good, so I made one up!"

Now I was deeply interested, wondering what my five-year-old had supposedly done over the past few months. This is how he began:

"Do you remember the time back in Canada when I was in that go-kart race and in the middle of the race my go-kart exploded and turned into a motorcycle and then I drove through the big red ribbon at the end and they gave me a big gold trophy?!"

I said, "No, I do not remember that."

But he wasn't upset. He simply put his hand on my forehead and closed his eyes. He waited a bit, then opened his eyes and looked into mine and said, "Do you remember now?"

What my son was after that day is in essence what we are all after in our lives: *a better story*. We want to live a story that is better than the one we so often end up living, which sounds like everyone else's story. It's like we are trapped in a small world with inevitable roles and vanilla outcomes.

The reason we want to live a better story is because we are

made to live a better story. What my son imagined that day was impossible, but there *are* better stories that are not only possible— they are essential for us to live.

Here's a story we could live right now: *men and women are better together.* This isn't some kind of slogan or Pollyanna think- ing. This is how we were made.

Men and women working well together could change the world. Literally. And that's not some big-idea kind of a thing. It's not even a small-stretch hyperbole—it's true. There is ample data to support it. World leaders, business owners, corporate think tanks, political experts, branding specialists, church-growth experts, and economic advisors have all chimed in to this dis- cussion with the same conclusions about what could change the future, and it's this: gender equity. Realizing true equality will require the empowerment of women. And empowering women will have an incredible impact on shaping a better future. We can step into the future together even now, as folks on the front lines of making a better world keep shouting out the answer! The economy, family, community, social issues, business—all of the drum majors of change call us to imagine with them what the world could be if women were truly empowered and could share in real equity as leaders of change.

It may be confusing to understand why empowerment is still necessary when equal rights have been won (well, in some countries). So a word about the relationship between equality and equity might help us understand the imperative of women's empowerment in the conversation about relationships between the sexes.

This is often a confusing concept. Equality has often been considered the goal when it comes to women's empowerment. When we reach equal "rights" (right to vote, go to school, equal pay, etc.), we think we've achieved equality. *But equal rights without equal opportunity is not really equality at all.* That's why equity is required and perhaps an even better aim.

Equity = rights + opportunity

Equal rights: the concept that every person is to be treated equally by the law

Equal opportunity: absence of discrimination, as in the workplace, based on race, color, age, gender, national origin, religion, or mental or physical disability

Equality: the condition of being equal, or the same in quality, measure, esteem, or value

Equity: fairness

Empowerment: the granting of political, social, or economic power to an individual or group; the process of supporting another person or persons to discover and claim personal power; the state of being empowered (either generally, or specifically)[1]

Equity is exercising fairness when it comes to equality. Think about a kid who gets a toy for Christmas. Let's say it's a remote-control car. If the car just sits in its box on the shelf and the kid can see it but never use it, what kind of gift is it? It's useless. It's not really a gift at all. At least it's not a gift that can be enjoyed or fully realized. Think about equality like that gift. The only way it can be truly appreciated, or received, is if the person who has it can use it.

In the 1970s symphony orchestras in America were mainly composed of men. It wasn't until 1980 that the top five professional groups went from fewer than 5 percent to 10 percent female musicians. By 1997, that number was up to 25 percent and it continues to rise. It wasn't that women did not have the right to play any orchestra instrument they wanted; it was that no matter how good they were, the auditions would almost always result in a man getting the position. Was it possible that men were better musicians than women? If they were not, then why were they consistently chosen above the women in the auditions? Good questions. The answer is about equity.

Orchestras determined they needed to find the source of the problem, so they began by changing the way they held auditions. In the 1980s they introduced the blind audition in which the musician played behind a screen so that the selection committee would choose the best based on the music alone. They could not see the musicians, only hear them (think *The Voice*). The result? More women were chosen. Researchers have determined that just this one adjustment, using the screen, made it 50 percent more likely for women to advance to the finals.[2]

Here's the thing: I don't think that the people selecting the musicians were blatantly sexist. I just think that culture had created a bias against women that effectively rendered their equality useless. The blind auditions were a way of exercising equity in the hiring process and had drastic results. Not only were more women able to achieve their potential but the orchestras also improved. Equity is the way we use equality toward a better world.

The Application of Equality

It's in the *application* of equality that we often lose our way. Equality is a right, but if you can't access that right, how is it helpful? Equality is a fight in itself, but equity is the experience of equality in everyday life. If, for instance, women have the "right" to equality but no access to use it, then equality is not what they actually have. It becomes an illusion. It's why women's empowerment is essential for them to achieve equity, because it's *how* equality will be realized in real life.

This is also why leaders in different spheres around the globe agree that women's empowerment will help equity be a real thing in our world. And equity (the application of equality in relationships) will change things for *everyone*. The orchestras do not regret their adjustments. They are better for it. And perhaps that's the missing point in the conversation around women's empowerment. This is not just about women—it's about all of us. Empowerment with equity will make us all better, together.

The Economic Impact

If money does the talking, let's start by listening to economic experts. According to the *Global Gender Gap Report* of 2017 issued by the World Economic Forum, "Gender parity is fundamental to whether and how economies and societies thrive. Ensuring the full development and appropriate deployment of half of the world's total talent pool has a vast bearing on the growth, competitiveness and future-readiness of economies and businesses worldwide."[3]

While all types of inequality have economic consequences, the McKinsey Global Institute report *The Power of Parity: How Advancing Women's Equality Can Add $12 Trillion to Global Growth* focuses on the economic implications of lack of parity between men and women: "A 'best in region' scenario, in which all countries match the rate of improvement of the fastest-improving country in their region could add as much as $12 trillion, or 11 percent, in annual 2025 GDP. In a 'full potential' scenario, in which women play an identical role in labor markets to that of men, as much as $28 trillion, or 26 percent, could be added to global annual GDP by 2025."[4]

If trillions of dollars could be added to our economy by making some adjustments that would not only add revenue but allow women more equality, then why don't we do it?

Power and Politics

In India, having women in at least 30 percent of local policy-making seats has had positive results in bringing about an "alternative vision of community development with the introduction of streetlights, clinics, libraries and public toilets." Due to the success at a local level, negotiations soon began to extend the concept to state and national levels.[5]

After a recent trip to Rwanda, Christine Amour-Levar, cofounder of Women on a Mission, shared what she witnessed:

> Two decades after the 1994 genocide that killed an estimated 800,000 people in one hundred days, the great untold story of Rwanda's rise is how women rebuilt the nation. On a recent visit to this tiny (26,338 square kilometres) landlocked country in the heart of Africa, I discovered a nation that has risen from the ashes of a civil war, to become one of the fastest growing economies in the African continent. . . .
>
> Seeing his country so devastated and broken because of the genocide, [President Paul] Kagame realised he needed the Rwandan women, who were the majority survivors of the genocide, to step up and fill the vacuum. A new constitution was passed in 2003 decreeing that 30% of parliamentary seats be reserved for women. The government also pledged that girls' education would be encouraged and that women would be given leadership roles in the community and in key institutions. Women soon blew past the 30% quota and today, with 64% of its seats held by women, Rwanda's parliament leads the world in female representation.[6]

Having women in power has been exponentially beneficial not just to women in Rwanda but to everyone. No one regrets the equity quota that helped Rwanda empower women to use their power politically.

Making Peace

Is it possible that women could also help make the world more peaceful? Laurel Stone, a researcher on conflict management, genocide prevention, and women's security, explained how involving women in peace-building increases the probability that violence will end by 27 percent. She said, "Institutionalising gender equality by ensuring female participation in the implementation of a peace plan and establishing gender electoral quotas can significantly increase the likelihood of peace lasting. For instance, implementing gender quotas for national legislatures could increase the probability of violence ending within five years by 27%."[7]

I read and watched and wept through the story of Leymah Gbowee from Liberia. A recipient of the Nobel Peace Prize, Gbowee is an example of what an empowered woman can do. In the midst of the Liberian civil war that seemed to never end, Gbowee organized some mothers who were tired of losing their children. Under harsh dictator Charles Taylor, boys were taken as child soldiers and girls were raped and murdered.

Tired of standing by and waiting for change, the mothers began to use the power they did have—their presence. Dressing in all white to signify their intentions toward peace, they began to pray in public spaces, openly defying the war with their public prayers. The movement began to grow as other women saw the power they could wield. Soon thousands of mothers dressed in white joined the movement to use nonviolence, prayer, and presence as a witness that they wanted a different future. Eventually this movement was instrumental in bringing a peace treaty to Liberia and taking down a tyrannical leader, which led to the election of the first female African president. These women didn't want to wield power for themselves, and they refused the idea that violence was the only way to make change.[8]

Research suggests that women included in peacekeeping negotiations can help to reduce potential conflict while they contribute to increased organizational stability. Women tend to create cultures that are more financially stable, healthier, and more humane in their treatment of each other while reducing corruption and crime.[9]

Nowhere was this more evident than through the lives of Liberian mothers under the leadership of Leymah Gbowee! Those women wanted to use every power they had for a better future for their children. When women use their power, more often than not, everyone benefits.

The Business Advantage

For business leaders, addressing barriers to gender equality can unlock new opportunities. In the World Economic Forum's 2016 *Future of Jobs Report*, for example, business leaders reported that addressing parity issues within their workforces could better match the changing gender composition of their customer base, and therefore enhance corporate decision-making and innovation.[10]

While improving workplace practices may require significant

effort in the short term, the subsequent long-term expansion of opportunities for women can transform company performance. Once again McKinsey & Company verifies that edge. They reported, "Our latest research finds that companies in the top quartile for gender or racial and ethnic diversity are more likely to have financial returns above their national industry medians."[11]

Many leading global companies are taking gender equity seriously, not because it's the right thing to do but because it's the smart thing to do. With competitive advantages through diversity, there has never been more need for informed corporate decision-making and business innovation. The 2017 *Global Gender Gap Report* showed that "companies with top quartile representation of women in executive committees have been shown to perform better than companies with no women at the top—by some estimates as much as a 47% premium on average return on equity." It's not just about making money, even though "more diverse leadership teams can cater to a broader array of stakeholder needs and concerns." Other benefits include corporate sustainability and growth in future markets.[12]

Human progress is a curious thing. It took about sixty years from first flight to put a man on the moon, but it will take over a hundred years to put a woman in the boardroom in many places on our planet. According to the 2018 *Global Gender Gap Report*, closing the global political gender gap is projected to take 107 years.[13]

The harsh realities of these projections are not just bad news for women; they should be a siren call for those who want to run better businesses and create a better world. Research suggests that women leaders in business make the entire company better. It's time to harness the gender advantage in every business.

Solving World Hunger

Every human being deserves the right to have access to adequate food. According to the World Food Program, "Eliminating inequalities between women and men farmers would increase agricultural production by 2.5 to 4 percent in developing countries, which translates to a 12 to 17 percent reduction in global hunger, or 100 to 150 million fewer hungry people."[14] Think about this for a minute. This is not just about securing the rights of women to work—this could end world hunger. The results of this study help explain the imperative of promoting gender equality, which involves "providing food assistance in ways that assign equal value to women and men while respecting their differences."[15]

To achieve food and nutrition security for all people without distinction, food-assistance policies and programs must create conditions that advance, rather than undermine, gender equality and women's empowerment.

Poverty Reduction

In 2006 Muhammad Yunus won a Nobel Peace Prize for the invention of microcredit. As founder of the Grameen Bank in Bangladesh, whose story is detailed in his book *Banker to the*

Poor, Yunus explained the bank's strategy was to end extreme poverty through microcredit to the poorest of the poor. When he took the time to really listen to the poorest of the poor, he found out how the oppression was working, and he began to unravel it by lending money to women. Empowering women, he discovered, was the best way to break the back of extreme poverty.

I remember how amazed I was at the acceptance speech he gave when he received his Nobel. He accepted it on behalf of his grandchildren. He said he couldn't wait to take his grandkids by the hand and visit the museum of extreme poverty to show them what it used to look like. Yunus was so convinced it was possible to end the oppression of poverty that he actually believed it and then lived it. Ninety-seven percent of the Grameen microcredit loans were given to women. Why? The returns for community development and the payback rates were good. Empowering women simply made the most impact.

Better Homes and Families

The research is gaining speed in this area, but all of it suggests that although women make up a much larger part of the working world, they still hold the vast majority of household responsibilities. This negatively affects their leadership capacity. It's not rocket science to figure out that if a woman is running a race with a backpack weighed down with responsibility, she's going to be slower. This is virtually how every woman who is bearing the brunt of household responsibilities is running her leadership race: with a weighted, heavy sack. The answer is not to drop the sack. I don't leave the sole responsibilities of the household to my husband. I don't even want to. I enjoy being a mother and caring for my family. The real long-term and transformative answer is to share the load. Equity at work is deeply connected to equity at home.

Not only is this a way of lightening the load of working women, but it's also the way of creating a holistic family life for men. As each partner does more of the household share, they grow in their capacity for love, inclusion, and involvement in the life of the family. The shared "load" of responsibility turns into a shared love. Not only is the load easier to bear; it becomes an entry point of connectedness and strength, modeling a shared leadership to the next generation.

Consider the poll results from a study about working women and the effects on family life: "The ability to plan families, gender-egalitarian marriages and social pressure to share in parenting together mean healthier kids, more involved parents, lower divorce rates and more stable families. Poll results like these, which show that career is important and good parenting even more so, reflect the fact that gender equality isn't the enemy of the family."[16]

While speaking at a conference in Switzerland, I heard an interview with the town mayor, who was a woman, and her husband, who was a doctor. The interviewer was intrigued as to how they worked out their marriage with the woman holding a seemingly more important, public role. The woman pointed out that no one ever asks a man about this, but she answered anyway!

She shared how they were both committed to using their gifts in whatever way God directed them. God made it very clear to both of them that she had the gift of leadership and was called to politics. She was good at it. Because they saw this as an advance for everyone, they decided to adjust their family dynamics to make it possible. The husband hired some other physicians for his practice so he could leave early and be home after school for the kids. They created some strategies for dinner and meal prep and built flexibility into their family plan. The most powerful part of the interview wasn't just the practical nature of the adjustments they made for everyone to thrive but the testimony of her husband. He could not have predicted the incredible benefits in the new arrangements. He said he could not have realized how much he was missing out on the everyday activities of his children, but he was so thankful for the time after school and on the weekends when he was home with the kids. He had become a better father and a better man. He had expected the arrangements to cost him, and there were some small economic costs, but he was most surprised with the incredible payoff from being a dad who was available and involved in his kids' lives.

I loved hearing his surprise takeaway, and it resonated with me because of my own experience. I've seen my husband flourish and connect with our kids in a way I've rarely witnessed in the generation I grew up in. I can't help but think about the impact this has on him, our marriage, and our three boys.

Mutual involvement and shared household responsibilities with shared success at work mean a family unit that is strong and flexible—allowing everyone to flourish in whatever they are gifted to do. How beautifully liberating! Not only does this free me from a gender-specified role that limits my capacity depending on my gifting, but it frees my husband to be and do what he is called to as well—not just at work but at home. It frees my sons to function and flourish with two parents involved and present and actively engaged in the family. What a gift this is to our lives. And many more families would flourish if the shackles of gender roles were released from both women and men. It could be a surprising benefit to gender equity—but it shouldn't be. Surely by now we are sensing that when women and men are released to use their gifts, everyone benefits.

The Transformative Power of Equality

In virtually every sector of society, everyone benefits from the empowerment of women. Former UN Secretary General Kofi Annan noted, "Study after study has taught us, there is no tool for development more effective than the empowerment of women. No other policy is as likely to raise economic productivity or to reduce child and maternal mortality. No other policy is as sure to improve nutrition and promote health, including the prevention of HIV/AIDS. No other policy is as powerful in increasing the chances of education for the next generation."[17]

If you weren't convinced at the start of this chapter, I hope you are convinced by now. The case of women's empowerment is not some liberal agenda; it's a way of unlocking the potential that exists in everyone to flourish. Mutual thriving is what we are after, and when women get better, everyone gets better.

THREE

The Truth About Oppression

In the nineteenth century, the central moral challenge was slavery. In the twentieth century, it was the battle against totalitarianism. We believe that in this century the paramount moral challenge will be the struggle for gender equality in the developing world.

—NICHOLAS D. KRISTOF AND
SHERYL WUDUNN IN *HALF THE SKY*

So how is it possible that we know (through study, research, evidence, and experience) that when women flourish, everyone benefits, yet we remain stuck in old patterns of gender inequity? I'm glad you asked.

Acknowledging we have a shared future, we can now imagine a different world—one in which we are convinced that empowerment is key to mutual flourishing. But to find our way to the future, we have to locate ourselves in the here and now. Even a Google map has to know where you are starting to help you get where you want to go.

So where are we? In many respects we are stalled. According to research, hierarchies remain male dominated: "Only 21.8% of members of parliament are female . . . and of the 196 nations across the world, only 22 are led by women. . . . Although women comprise 47.3% of the US labor force, the percentage of women occupying top leadership positions, such as Fortune 500 CEOs, remains quite low—5.2 percent."[1]

Although companies and nonprofits and churches and networks report that they are highly committed to gender diversity, it hasn't translated into actual progress. Only 5 percent of the five hundred CEOs on the 2016 Fortune 500 list are women (twenty-seven out of five hundred). One study pointed out that there were more CEOs named John than there were women CEOs! The reality is that men are two to three times more likely to hold senior management positions than women, and we've been living this reality for thirty years without any changes. Research shows that employers still hire men over women, even with the same qualifications. If they do hire women, it is often at a lower salary.[2]

Not only is gender equity stalled but the fear knob on men and women working together has been turned way up. We have entered the #MeToo era. What does that mean? It means the cat's out of the bag. The worms are out of the can. Pandora's box is open. We have entered into a time when we can't pretend or ignore the oppression of women. And before I get into the details of what all that means, I want to take a minute to affirm what a great thing it is to be here. Right now in this time. Crisis equals opportunity.

The Painful Truth

A good friend of mine put it like this: "The truth will set you free, but first it will tick you off." The truth hurts. Exposure is a difficult thing to endure—but to be sure, it's a lot better than suffering in silence. We cannot hide in ignorance. The sheer numbers of women who have used their voices to speak up about the oppression they have been living with for generations is a wave of truth big enough to never get us back to "normal."

This is not a women's issue. And that's a key component in changing it. For a wound to be healed it needs to be exposed—air has to get to it—and treatment needs to be applied. All of those possibilities exist only when we acknowledge the injury. Half the world is hurting.

In their book *Half the Sky*, Pulitzer Prize winners Nicholas D. Kristof and Sheryl WuDunn wrote about the stark reality of what they consider this generation's most pressing injustice: the oppression of women. They reminded us that "more girls have been killed in the last fifty years, precisely because they were girls, than men were killed in all the battles of the twentieth century. More girls are killed in this routine 'gendercide' in any one decade than people were slaughtered in all the genocides of the twentieth century."[3]

How did we get here? The reality is that the oppression of

women is often difficult to spot. Rather than a large catastrophic event that makes what is happening obvious and clear, the killing and discriminating of women around the world has been more like a stealthy, dangerous undercurrent leading us slowly, yet inevitably, to death. A steady drift to where we never intended to go yet find ourselves nonetheless. Globally, the reality of oppression for women is dire. For Western countries like America, it's easy to assume it's better news. And to be sure, Western democracies have made it illegal to oppress women, legislated to protect the rights of women, and made it possible for women to speak up. But the stark reality is that women are still oppressed. The inequality and systemic abuse of women runs deep. It's global. And the exposure has come. The crisis is here. And with it, an unprecedented opportunity.

When the #MeToo hashtag was created, it wasn't a huge sensation. Originally started as a grassroots effort by activist Tarana Burke in 2006, it suddenly went viral after the hashtag was used by actress Alyssa Milano on October 15, 2017. Milano urged victims of sexual abuse to share their stories on Twitter after Hollywood power broker Harvey Weinstein was outed for his sexually abusive behaviors over decades.

Over nineteen million tweets hashtagged #MeToo in a year. It felt like the walls were falling down on the male establishment. After Weinstein's public outing, others quickly followed. It was as though women, collectively, were finally able to speak up and tell the truth. To be heard. To find and use their voice. To express their outrage and pain.

There was something refreshing about it—something

cathartic about all the pain that had been bottled up for so many generations finally being let out. There was something powerful about the collective nature of social media and the sheer courage of so many survivors telling their stories. As each person began to show such courage, it emboldened many more to speak their truth, and before anyone could really even understand what was going on, we were here. In the #MeToo era. Now we know that no one is immune to the realities of the deep wound of gender oppression in this generation.

The outpouring went beyond #MeToo in general to include men and women from Christian backgrounds and communities sharing their experiences of abuse in the church using the online hashtag #ChurchToo. No one was immune from the stinging truth of the social media tidal wave. Leaders, pastors, counselors, husbands, and fathers were called out on manipulation and abuse. It was time for some uncomfortable truth.[4]

As #MeToo put courage in the hearts of women, it put fear in the hearts of many men. But what was really going on?

Knowing the Real Problem

Come with me back in time. It's twenty-five years ago and I'm in a remote northern part of a Canadian national park as part of the staff of a survival camp. I know I said remote, but let me repeat that. It was *very* remote. It required driving several hours north of Toronto to Algonquin Provincial Park, then taking a small motorboat on a private lake to get to the site. Even bears get lost trying to find the place. At this particular time I was in love with Steve, my future husband, who was living in Toronto, a large metropolitan city. And Steve was in love with me. I knew this because he would make that long drive and take that onerous boat ride to visit me on my weekends off. Did I mention he was a city boy? Seriously. His idea of a good time is staying put with air-conditioning and great Wi-Fi. But love makes you do crazy things.

One weekend Steve and I decided to join a group of friends who were going to surf down some natural rapids in small inner tubes. It was crazy fun. Somewhere along the way Steve noticed that his foot was hurting. He figured he must have sprained it walking back up the rapids. When we got to the cabin, he was limping pretty badly, so he sat down and put his foot up. Someone brought some ice, but his foot continued to swell. He took some painkillers and headed back the next day to his job in the city, but his foot just kept throbbing and swelling. Steve kept up the routine—elevating it, icing it, and taking Tylenol while telling himself to suck it up and shake it off. After all, it wasn't his first sprained ankle.

Eventually the throbbing got a little out of control and Steve went to the doctor. The doctor took one look and told him that he had gotten there just in time. Another week and he might have died! Steve was shocked! How could that be? He had never heard of someone dying of a sprained ankle before. The doctor laughed, agreed, and said, "No, no one dies of a sprained ankle. The thing is, the problem isn't your ankle. The problem is the tiny cut under your big toe." Steve had evidently pricked his foot on a sharp rock while riding or walking back up the rapids. Bacteria from the water had entered the cut and gotten into his blood system. *And it was killing him.*

He was released with a prescription for antibiotics and in a few days was healthy, happy, and ready for another trip to the middle of nowhere to bond with the love of his life. Love really can kill you, it seems.

The warning embedded in the story is not about excursions on rapids in the wilderness. It's about treating the wrong problem. When it comes to movements such as #MeToo occurring within society, I believe we are tempted to treat the wrong thing. We can suggest the abuse is a management issue or a personality issue or an isolated issue or . . . the list can go on. Often we suggest that it's a "women's issue" and move on. But the truth is it's a human issue. It's an issue that runs straight to the heart of the brokenness at the center of humanity.

We can spend years restructuring or rebranding, even rehiring, but if we don't get to the source, we won't get better. The source of the problem is gender inequity; it's oppression. Like bacteria, sexism has entered our collective body and we are dying from the infection. The time for a proper diagnosis has come.

Many times when we are scared and hurt, we blame the person who is at the other end of the pain. In this case the people at the other end of the pain are women. The temptation is to believe that women are the problem. Or even to believe that the #MeToo movement or the #ChurchToo movement or the #SilenceIsntSpiritual campaign is the problem. But that would be treating an infection as though it were a broken ankle. It won't do anything, and even worse, it could lead to death.

If the recent social media campaigns aren't the problem, then what is? Gender inequity, which many times results in sexual violence and abuse, is the problem. The social movements that exposed the violence were the tip of the spear that revealed the real issue. Now to be sure, violence against women *is* a global problem that needs to be addressed! But under the surface of gender violence is an even more sinister reality that needs proper attention: it's inequality (the lack of equity). It's a present reality of the systemic oppression that faces women around the world. And it's not just about when someone is violated or sexually abused (although that is often when we might pay attention). It's more pervasive, and the consequences are much more acute in everyday life. Think about the kids, families, husbands, employees, bosses, companies, and governments affected. The impact of gender inequality is a reality too huge to ignore.

This is the root of the issue. The negative fruit that inequality has borne is visible. We see it and it smells bad. It looks ugly. We identify it, name it, and step back with sincere disgust and cry out against the violence.

But can we see the more invisible nature of attitudes, prejudices, and systemic realities that are working against women around the world? Can we see that when women are treated unfairly, not only do they suffer but all of us suffer? That's why this current crisis is an incredible opportunity. We don't have to keep walking around in pain anymore. We can finally stop putting our foot up like we have a sprained ankle when we are actually dying of an infection.

The fundamental relationship between the genders is broken.

And to repair it will take a proper diagnosis. This is the great opportunity we are living in right now. Once we know the real problem, we can treat it! And that treatment plan holds the possibility of making us whole again.

Understanding Oppression

Knowing where we are going allows us to imagine a future without oppression. But this is not an invitation to deny oppression. Allan G. Johnson once wrote, "We won't end oppression by pretending it isn't there or that we don't have to deal with it."[5] Recognizing the opportunity that this crisis affords us involves a willingness to understand the oppression that is facing us.

America was a racially charged nation in 1966 when Bobby Seale and Huey Newton founded the Black Panthers. A political organization intent on self-defense and arming citizens to monitor the behavior of police officers, they were responsible for many violent skirmishes and fatal firefights.

It was during their rise in influence that Martin Luther King Jr. was finding considerable success as a civil rights crusader. King couldn't understand why the blacks in the North didn't believe his nonviolent solutions would work for them. He challenged them on their ideas of violent overthrow and revolution. They responded that he just didn't understand the dilemma they faced in the northern states. He begged to differ. I mean the man had *already* won a Nobel Peace Prize, led a successful civil rights campaign, and was the spokesman for a nation. He asked them to explain it to him.

The men told him that the nature of oppression in the southern states was explicit. You could see it. You could name it. You could face it. But the oppression in the North was different. It was implicit. You were "free," just not free enough to get a job. You weren't owned by anyone, but you couldn't buy a house or move out of the inadequate housing. You were a father, but you couldn't provide for your family. It was an oppression that secretly circled the wagons all the while saying the words, "You are free here." And it was infuriating because it couldn't be named or confronted or seen. So Martin Luther King Jr. *moved* to Chicago, into a housing development three days a week, in an attempt to really understand what it was like.

Let me emphasize that last sentence. King *moved* from Atlanta, Georgia, center of the southern civil rights movement and his family home, to Chicago (*after* he had already won a Nobel Peace Prize) to *understand* the conditions and oppression of his brothers and sisters in the northern part of America.

Muhammad Yunus, the microloan Nobel Peace Prize recipient we discussed earlier, left his employment as an economic advisor to the government of Bangladesh and spent an entire year trying to understand why his financial reforms weren't changing the lives of the beggars he would see on the street. He met with the poorest people he could find so he could understand how poverty was oppressing his country. He believed that if he could learn how oppression worked, he could help undo it.

Transformational leaders turn crises into opportunities. And to do that they do everything they can to understand the problem. Understanding how oppression works is an essential part of undoing it.

To really understand oppression means we have to move. For you it might not require taking a year off of your full-time employment or moving to another part of the country, but it will require movement. You might have to move your position, move your prejudice, move to a different perspective, move your attention, move your priorities, or move your posture. But here's the deal: if you change nothing, nothing will change. Take a page out of the lives of transformational leaders who used crisis as an opportunity and did whatever they could to truly understand oppression so they could begin the long and beautiful work of undoing it.

FOUR

A Vision for Reconciliation

Truth can be told in an instant, forgiveness can be offered spontaneously, but reconciliation is the work of lifetimes and generations.

—KRISTA TIPPETT IN *SPEAKING OF FAITH*

On a recent visit to Rwanda, I was speaking to a man who was an advisor to the Rwandan government and a Christian leader before and after the genocide. He was telling me about the reality of the church in Rwanda. He told me that the Sunday before the genocide, 92 percent of Rwandans were in church. After it was all over, he wondered how he would ever preach again. What could the church say? How could they gather people in churches that had been part of and complicit in such a great injustice? But it wasn't long before he understood what they needed to say. The possibility of a new future soon dawned on them.

Rwandans needed a place to go with their grief. With their sorrow. They needed a place of healing. Someone to help them carry their suffering. Other Rwandans needed a place to go with their shame. With their guilt. With the blood on their hands. They needed to find some forgiveness. *Where can people go for that?* What can reach that depth of pain and stain of guilt? This is when the church in Rwanda began to discover the relevance and power of what Christians believe to be the center of their faith: the cross. They began to preach the gospel by telling people about what Jesus had done on the cross.

This is so important for us right now. It's not the church that is the answer, and we know that now. We watch in dread as church leaders are named and shamed and church structures and attitudes side with oppression. We watch in shame as those who are guilty are shunned from the very places they might find forgiveness and restoration. We're stunned as Christian leaders have been exposed as complicit in the destruction of healthy relationships between women and men. *The church without the centrality of the cross is just a community group.* But the cross, that is where true power is on display for the deepest wounds of the world. The deepest wounds in us. When it comes to deep-seated injustices, there is only one place to go that might lead to healing and unravel the oppression that has held us all. There is only one place to go that might spur us to the hope of a different future, to change, to repentance and forgiveness and reconciliation. It's the cross.

Jesus embraced the cross as a demonstration of love and power personified. It is power to break the back of sin, shame, guilt, fear, and death. And it is love to soothe and heal shame, suffering, abuse, and pain. It is the place of transformation.

No matter who we are, the oppressor or the oppressed, we will find what we need to get free from oppression's tragic cycle. We will find this freedom in the person of Jesus on the cross. On the cross Jesus reconciled the whole world to himself. C. S. Lewis described how when Jesus died on the cross, time itself began to move backward.[1] What he meant was that creation could now be restored to everything God had originally created it to be. When we think of the consequences of humans acting selfishly, we can follow a trajectory that began in the Genesis story of broken relationships. First between humanity and God. Then between men and women. Then between siblings, then between tribes, and this repeats itself until we find ourselves at this point in time, in a world tragically divided. What is the remedy?

It's a transformational idea to suggest that our restored relationship with God would begin to restore our relationships with everything and everyone else. Indeed, it's the gospel. A good description of the gospel itself is the "ministry of reconciliation."[2] Can we imagine a reconciled world? I think right relationships are good news for this life.

To be reconciled means that our relationships are made right. But relationships that are broken need repair. And repair takes effort and time. The righting of broken relationships (reconciliation) needs some guidance. Too often we think that powerful spiritual things happen by "magic." But they don't. They happen through grace and loads of work. The work of reconciliation has a pattern—some stages to follow that might just lead us to resilient relationships in our own lives. Let's have a look at what forgiveness is, what it's not, and how true repentance will help us move toward reconciliation.

Forgiveness Opens the Door to Personal Freedom

Forgiveness is the only path to freedom. It is best described as the internal process of releasing bitterness. Forgiveness is what enables the victims of abuse to move forward in their lives. Forgiveness is a doorway to hope and a helping agent of healing. Forgiveness is a way out of the prison of fear.

People who struggle with memories and fear and ongoing bitterness and resentment need to explore the possibility of forgiveness as a way of healing and a path to freedom. This can take time. And practice. Often a choice to forgive someone will need to be made many times over. You may need some professional help to unlock this door. Forgiveness is definitely a spiritual decision and will require spiritual power. Begin to pray and ask God to move your heart toward forgiveness.

Desmond Tutu wrote a book called *No Future Without Forgiveness*. In it he tells the amazing story of establishing the Truth and Reconciliation Commission in South Africa. Both Nelson Mandela and Tutu understood at a deeply personal level that forgiveness would be necessary for there to be any possibility of a shared future in their country. Bitterness, resentment, and unforgiveness are too heavy to carry into a new future. But we all suffer from some misconceptions about forgiveness that keep us wary of using it as a tool of liberation.

To Forgive Does Not Mean to Forget

Forgiveness does not mean that everything is okay. My youngest son often responds this way when his older brother is forced to apologize for something he did wrong. His brother will apologize, and the little guy will almost always respond, "It's okay."

But I stop him every time. I remind them both that it's actually *not okay*. "It's not okay to treat your brother that way," I remind my older son. "And it's not okay that he did that to you," I say to the younger. But I remind them both that the power of forgiveness is exercising your choice about how you will respond. Because it's not okay, you can choose what you are going to do about it. Forgiveness is less about dismissing wrong and more about letting the wrong go. Forgiveness is a choice.

It is also important to understand that forgiveness is not reconciliation. Reconciliation of broken relationships is not solely for the injured party to pursue. They have already endured the abuse. This is often one of the hardest parts of being the victim: the inability you have to reconcile the relationship. And this is what makes reconciliation so profound. It cannot be done alone. Right relationships require reciprocity to truly heal. This is a work we can only do together. Isn't that amazing? We practice flourishing together by the process of dealing with our past wrongs together.

Repentance Is Required

Reconciliation is not possible without repentance. This is where the restoration of relationships between women and men and everyone else can get difficult. Repentance is required. Repentance is the acknowledgment of the wrong done and an expressed willingness to make it right. Without repentance there is no reconciliation. There really isn't any restoration either. Men who have abused need to take responsibility for their actions: confess them (acknowledge the behavior) and repent of them (express genuine remorse and regret) and be *willing* to do what it takes to make things right. This might include paying for counseling for the victim, public apologies, or helping lead other men to freedom from abusive cycles.

When I was visiting Rwanda, I sat with a survivor (Grace) and a perpetrator (John) of the genocide. Grace had survived but her entire family had been slaughtered. She quickly introduced us to her neighbor, who was sitting on her left. He was a friend *and* was also the one who had slaughtered her family. We all took a deep breath. They told us their story together.

First they told us they were now neighbors and good friends. Then we bombarded them with questions. All of our questions were basically the same: How can that even be possible? They were honest. It wasn't some shallow, Pollyanna, "it's okay" kind of restoration. Grace spoke of dealing with her own pain. Of wanting to die. Of getting personal and group therapy. Of taking her time. Of choosing to let go of bitterness as a way of coping. She spoke of releasing her anger, but she also shared about how the fear never left. She was terribly afraid. Then John spoke. He told us of being in prison and in a prison even darker still—the inside of his guilt. He spent years with the deep, dark reality of what he had done sinking into his spirit. He hated himself. He wanted to die. He knew he deserved it. He was so ashamed that he would never look anyone in the eye.

A visitor came to the prison camp John was in and announced the opportunity for prisoners to participate in a reconciliation project. It would result in prisoners having their sentence reduced by half but would require a full admission of guilt, a telling of everything they knew (including the names of perpetrators not yet found and the placement of dead bodies for the necessary grieving process of victims), and the willingness to make amends in whatever way possible. John didn't think he was a candidate to participate. But he also knew that if he didn't change something on the inside of him, he would not just be in prison longer; he would be lost forever. He put up his hand. He wept as he told the details of his crimes. He wrote letters to Grace. Even in prison, he started to work on "cleanup" brigades to help rebuild the nation. He told his story to others and spoke often of his desire to make things right. He got counseling and group therapy and started to *take responsibility not only for what he had done wrong but for what he could do right.*

Soon both Grace and John were invited to move into a village of reconciliation. The government was creating new communities of victims and perpetrators as a way to rebuild the country on the principles of "one people." These villages are like cities on a hill for Rwanda. Possibilities of a shared future after such a horrific past. People don't need lectures on reconciliation—they need examples.

The actual way their relationship began to heal is worth repeating. They were given a shared plot of land, which they quickly divided in half. Grace spoke of her constant fear of having to be so close to the man who had taken so much from her. John shared his constant fear of having to face the woman he had wronged. Petrified but committed, they started to build their own houses. There was a pile of bricks in the middle of the property, and they would see each other only occasionally if they happened to get their bricks at the same time. The encounters were awkward and filled with fear for Grace and shame for John. They both dreaded them. Grace would finish for the day, but John would stay. He would stay to work on Grace's house. Maybe at first he couldn't face Grace, but he could serve her. In her absence, he would work on her house, paying careful attention to the detail. Brick by brick he would demonstrate his repentance.

That's how the work of restoration goes, if we are honest: brick by brick. Soon, Grace and John would meet at the brick pile, not by accident, but on purpose. Both of them confronting the demons of their past. Grace would ask John for some advice and John would be quick to not only offer it but to do it as well. The fear started to fade in Grace's mind. The shame started to quiet in John's heart. They discovered they liked each other's company. They slowly saw beyond the past and into the future. They were reconciling. Both Grace and John emphasized how much time this took. How much effort. How much work it was to dig deeper than fear and shame. They didn't sugarcoat it. And I'm thankful.

This is the work of reconciliation. It requires everyone to do what they can toward the possibility of a shared future.

Reconciliation Is Forgiveness + Repentance

If there is forgiveness (victim based) and repentance (abuser based), there is the *possibility* of reconciliation. But it's not always the best option. Sometimes, depending on the type of abuse and the personal situation of the parties involved, reconciliation is not possible or even advised. Sometimes it will take a long time for the reality of restoration to be realized. What is for sure is that the cross is the only place we can meet. And the cross is our only hope of restored relationships. These days when I think of the cross, I see a whole pile of bricks at the foot of it. Men and women will need to meet there to build a new future. And our future will be built together, brick by brick.

Keeping the cross at the center of our strategy for a transformed future is the only way we can achieve it. I talked to dozens of survivors of the genocide in Rwanda. I asked every one of them how they went on to live, how they could possibly forgive, how they could commit to reconciliation, and they all answered the same: Jesus. Jesus is the only way to a shared and transformed future. The cross offers us a solid place to stand in the sinking reality of our brokenness. When we are tired of the journey, we can always find our way to the cross for stamina. When we are weary and discouraged, we can always find our way to the cross for persevering hope. When we are overwhelmed with guilt and our complicity in oppression, we can find our way to the cross for forgiveness. When we uncover truths of our own wounds, we can find our way to the cross for healing. Rather than a step on the journey of transformation, the cross functions more like a compass. The cross is true north for pilgrims on a journey to the future.

For a reconciled future, women and men will need to visit the cross, to see the life of Jesus, then allow his life to transform us and invite us toward creating a better world together. Every action we take at the foot of the cross is either a push forward toward a better future or a pull back to crisis and oppression. I'm praying that the cross will be the starting place and we will join together to push forward toward realizing a thriving future for all of us.

PART TWO

Where We Find Ourselves

FIVE

How We Feel

The Pull Back of Fear,

the Push Forward of Action

I never worry about action, but only inaction.

—Winston Churchill

I can feel the fear. I feel it every time another #MeToo gets posted and the growing voices of women rise to a collective pitch that cries for change. Every time another man is exposed for sexual harassment, held trial by a public inquiry that is angry and demanding justice. Every time the culture from even one generation ago is dragged into the daylight of our current values. Fear.

I spoke with a business leader recently who is paralyzed in his hiring process because he feels terrified about making a wrong choice in a culture that is rife with hypersensitivity to gender and color and sexuality. He does not know what to do because he is afraid. And he is not alone. A young up-and-coming woman entering the workforce is sexually harassed on a business retreat by a senior partner in the firm. She is shaken and humiliated and calls her friend to pick her up early. She debriefs the experience and knows deep within that she should probably make a formal complaint for the sake of women coming after her, but she also thinks that it really wouldn't matter. She feels silenced, ashamed, afraid, and, well, paralyzed.

Decision Paralysis

Decision paralysis happens when we don't know what to do so we decide to do nothing. We freeze. Rather than make the wrong decision, we make no decision. By definition, paralysis is "the loss of the ability to move some or all of the body."

We convince ourselves that doing nothing will buy us time and stall the inevitable changes that are necessary. But it doesn't. Doing nothing is an action. It cements the ways of the status quo and creates a paralysis that prevents any change from emerging.

Sometimes we think paralysis is inevitable and we feel helpless in the power of its grip. But it isn't. Believe it or not, even physical paralysis has been overcome. New methods of neurological design have learned to bypass the broken spinal systems in paralyzed patients and help them walk again. In 2015 such a situation happened in California with Adam Fritz. At twenty-one,

Adam had a motorcycle accident that led to a spinal cord injury that left him paralyzed in both legs. Fritz should have spent his life in a wheelchair. But he didn't. His tenacity to keep working toward walking again (he went to the gym at least four times a week to keep active) was matched by the genius of biomedical engineering professor Zoran Nenadic.

Nenadic and his team tapped into the part of the brain that wasn't affected by a spinal cord injury. Fritz's injury was to the neural connection to his legs, but the brain region that initially sends the signal to move his legs wasn't damaged. "Find a way to bypass the damaged region in the spine and send electrical stimulation directly to the muscles, and a patient could walk again just by thinking about it," *Time* reported. "Fritz, who was supposed to spend his life in a wheelchair, is back on his feet, thanks to an elaborate combination of virtual reality, computer algorithms and a whole lot of ingenuity."[1]

Think about it. This is incredible. Although difficult to believe, and even more difficult to accomplish, *it is possible*. Through *thinking* a different way, a whole lot of work, new technology, and some outside-the-box activities, a man who was paralyzed can walk again.

I think the same kind of moment exists for those of us who think that *women and men working together is too hard*. Why? Because we live in the kind of world that can attack paralysis with new ways of thinking. New technology. New systems and structures. New exercises. Real things that translate into new ways of living. The central point is that losing hope, giving up, and accepting paralysis as the only option is false. Not only is it not the *only* option, but it's a *terrible* option. Especially when it's the fear of failing that is paralyzing us. Don't get me wrong; I'm not suggesting it's easy. Ask Fritz and I'm sure he will tell you it can be agonizing. But he will also tell you that to do nothing is to be stuck forever. If you change nothing, nothing changes.

Jeff Lockyear is a senior pastor in Canada. His church believes women should and can lead. The problem for them was that no women did. They thought it was a good, biblically sound decision for women's empowerment to be practiced both in the world and at their church, but their church culture didn't change. Just because they came to believe women should be leading didn't translate into women leading. When they looked honestly at the culture of their church leadership, it was a boys' club. They wanted it to change, but it didn't.

For a while they scratched their heads and believed a bit harder. But again, nothing happened. Then they got curious about why their beliefs weren't making any tangible difference. That's when God connected them to Ellen Duffield, the director of a leadership ministry in Canada who'd been doing PhD-level research on female engagement and empowerment.

It wasn't until the church leadership began to make an action plan and work it out in their local context that anything began to shift.

What did they do? They got help. I asked Jeff what the secret was to the cultural shift in gender leadership at his church, and he said it was simple: investment and invitation. Once they identified the problem, they acted on the solutions. Jeff explained, "In the process of five years of disproportionate investment and disproportionate invitation, we've seen God move in some breath-taking ways. Today we have female elders and a female board chair. Our staff is now 50 percent women represented by a senior leadership of 50 percent women. Women hold power and are visible role models."[2]

Once they started to act on their beliefs, a lot changed in their church culture and leadership team. When you speak with Jeff, he is very excited and so is the leadership team at his church. Sure, they are thrilled that they were able to confront their fears and create a new culture, but they are even more excited about the future! Jeff talks about this subject with a huge smile because, as he explained it to me, it's changed the way he thinks about the future of his own daughter and the capacity he is building for her to become all that she is gifted to be. And she's only nine. But are you catching the idea here? His excitement didn't exist when he simply believed that gender equity was the ideal but didn't act on it. He was still stuck in a world of "believing" that never affected real life because there was no action. Jeff is excited because he decided to do something.

Using Our Differences as a Strength

To act on our belief will require us to confront our fears. How do we confront the fear of men and women to work together in equitable relationships? Seth Richardson, an Anglican rector in Fayetteville, Arkansas, suggested it can be done by holding two concepts in balance—difference and mutuality.

Let's start with this beautiful question: "What if shared leadership between men and women is *not* inherently dangerous?" Seth asked this question in his article "Is (Healthy) Cross-Gendered Ministry Even Possible?" He wrote, "Rather than perpetuate broken hierarchies that wound and dehumanize, a model for shared ministry characterized by difference and mutuality can bring healing and hope."[3] I agree.

I was once the president of the ministerial association in a small town in northern Canada. The association was between the pastors of the town and had loosely functioned as a way of getting the church leaders together. It was nice. I had a vision that the association could be a lot more strategic. What if we could build great relationships between our churches and also a great strategy? How could the churches work together to bring transformation to the community? That was the dominant question on my mind.

I had heard some stories of transformation in communities around the world, and I thought our town would be a perfect place to try them out. I proposed the idea to the group, was promptly elected president, and we got to work. We mapped out the town and identified the various church "areas" and prayed with one another. We signed a covenant of relationship that spelled out that we were "with each other" and "for each other." We promised not to entertain anyone or anything that would break trust between us. We decided we wouldn't celebrate our own church growth if the whole church (in the whole city) didn't also grow. We tied our successes together. We identified a watermark level for city-wide church attendance and activity and then measured it yearly and celebrated as it grew. We identified areas of deep need in the community and struck up a church-based plan to meet the needs. It was an incredible time. The community began to see the church leading from relationship and unity—a shared leadership model—no longer competing with one another but collaborating for others.

Because it was my first post as a Christian leader, I assumed this kind of thing was normal. I had no other experience to compare it to. One day, a few years into this effort, a member of the ministerial association from a denomination that didn't welcome women leaders came up to me and said, "Isn't it amazing that you have been leading this *as a woman*?" He wasn't trying to be dismissive; he was genuinely surprised. He was celebrating the audacity of it.

The thing is, I hadn't even given that a thought. I remember thinking to myself, *I'm a woman?* It wasn't that I was having some sort of dysfunctional identity crisis; it was just that I had not thought of myself with my gender *first* before. I had always thought of myself as a church leader in this context, doing my best to unite the churches and impact the community. I honestly had not thought of being a *woman* church leader until that moment.

I've been thinking about this scenario a lot as I've been researching this book. I believe that if I had viewed my leadership through the lens of difference of gender alone, I wouldn't have mentioned my vision. Gender is such a loaded area of difference in light of culture, fear, experience, confusion, and pain that if we view it separately or even dominantly, it will distort everything else.

Now, I don't mean that difference should be ignored. I do not believe every human is the same. I don't believe that women are the same as men or that men are the same as women. I also do not think that all women are the same as other women or that all men are the same as other men. Humans, by definition, are different. We are unique. Every human is distinctive and equal. Equality does not mean sameness. Equality means we are all worthy, not identical. And humans are equal in the fact that they are different from any other human. I was just having a conversation with my sons about how old they are when their fingerprints are formed. They are not even out of the womb when their identities are already completely unique. To be different is to be human. So how is it that our difference became so problematic?

Difference
dif·fer·ence
/ˈdif(ə)rəns/
noun
difference; plural noun: differences
a point or way in which people or things are not the same

Distorting Our Difference

You might not have heard of Jane Elliott. Ms. Elliott was a school teacher who was particularly impacted by the death of Martin Luther King Jr. in 1968. She was tired of racism winning, so she decided to do what she could with what she had. And what she had was a third-grade classroom full of white rural kids in America. She embarked on creating a lesson that would turn into a social experiment called "Blue Eyes / Brown Eyes." It's controversial and quite shocking, but it sheds light on how difference, although a natural human quality, can turn into a system of rejection and fear.

Ms. Elliott divided her class into two sections. One had blue eyes and the other had brown. For the first day she set out privileges for the blue-eyed children after she explained they were superior to their peers. The blue-eyed kids received an extra-long lunch break and an extra recess and were praised for being so gifted and smart. The brown-eyed kids were reminded of their inferior status and were restricted during recess. The next day she reversed the scene. She told the kids the latest evidence was just the opposite of yesterday. To the blue-eyed kids' horror, the brown-eyed kids prevailed as the ruling class of the classroom. Even though the experiment was one day for each eye color, the results were extraordinarily disturbing. Jane Elliott described it: "I watched what had been marvelous, cooperative, wonderful, thoughtful children turn into nasty, vicious, discriminating, little third-graders in a space of fifteen minutes."[4]

But it wasn't only the racism that was surprising. The results of the kids' tests and answers and class participation all corresponded to the way they valued themselves. Elliott remembered, "I use phonics. We use the card pack, and the children, the brown-eyed children were in the low class the first day and it took them five and a half minutes to get through the card pack. The second day it took them two and a half minutes. The only thing that had changed was the fact that now they were superior people."[5]

The kids who were sitting in the seats of superior eye color performed better, and the reverse was also true. The point of the exercise was to show how easy it was to use a difference and distort it to form the basis of prejudice.

A video by PBS followed up fourteen years later. The kids who had participated in the experiment were now adults. The filmmakers wondered how they were doing and what they thought about the class experiment now. They all watched the original video together showing the two-day experiment and then talked about their own involvement and how it influenced the way they live. The video shows grown adults who experienced both being racist and being a target of racism during the third grade. They tell of how short the experiment was but how lasting its impact. They managed to see and feel the connection between taking differences and distorting them to become tools of oppression. Because most of the children had lived and played together before the experiment, it offered an incredible window into the power of leadership to determine behavior.[6]

Difference Out of Proportion

This reminds me of that enlightening trip to Rwanda. I was visiting the country on an immersive peacekeeping trip with Amplify Peace and World Relief. Twenty-five years ago Rwanda faced the unthinkable when the country descended into a bloodbath. Eight hundred thousand people were massacred in a little over a month. In total 1.2 million Rwandans died, a million fled the country, and 150,000 perpetrators of the violence were in custody. I asked how something this tragic could happen and was told there was no simple explanation, that what happened in Rwanda was a complex and multilayered phenomenon. But if I needed a simple answer, it could be boiled down to simply accentuating differences. Overemphasizing our differences will always lead to violence. Let that sink in.

When we take one difference and emphasize it out of proportion with our other wonderful human differences, we digress toward prejudice. It's that simple. Sexism works the exact same way.

Using difference as a metric without mutuality distorts everyone's views. Men can view women as "less than," but women can also view themselves that way. The truth is that if we look at difference through the lens of fear and suspicion, it will always lead to oppression. But what if difference wasn't something to fear? What if it was a gift rather than a threat?

Seth Richardson suggested there is a way to expose and confront the fear-based approach to men and women in leadership together by using a "positive model characterized by difference and mutuality."[7]

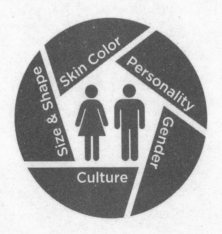

Viewing difference through the lens of fear will have a whole heap of negative results:

Blatant prejudice: assigning value based on gender alone (men are superior / women are inferior)

Stereotypes: all women are alike / all men are alike

Tokenism: quick and easy gender-based positions that don't change culture or contribute to a solution

Denial of difference: believing there is no difference; a denial of our humanity

Gender is a difference, but it is only one difference among many. It is not the only or even the most important distinction. When we see each other only through the gender lens, we over-emphasize that one distinction, and it distorts our ability to see each other as humans. But we can confront our fear and approach difference with imagination and faith. Then we quickly discover difference as an opportunity and gift, which leads us to mutuality.

Mutuality
mu·tu·al·i·ty
/ˌmyo͞oCHə ˈwalədē//
noun
the sharing of a feeling, action, or relationship between two
or more parties

The Beauty of a Shared Humanity

Mutuality is what made Nelson Mandela decide to build a new
nation under the African tribal principle of *ubuntu*.

> *Ubuntu* (Zulu pronunciation: [ùɓúnt'ù]) is a Nguni Bantu term
> meaning "humanity." It is often translated as "I am because
> we are," or "humanity towards others," but is often used in a
> more philosophical sense to mean "the belief in a universal
> bond of sharing that connects all humanity."[8]

Fortune magazine took a look at this principle of Mandela's
leadership and called it "alignment." Rather than focusing on
difference, Mandela emphasized mutuality.

He understood rallying the country and bridging diverse
interests meant making room for others. Black supremacy
was as depraved as white supremacy, in his view. Mandela
knew that over a billion people would watch his inaugural

presidential address and used this speech—and key plural pronouns *we, us,* and *our*—to align a deeply divided nation around a common vision: "We understand it still that there is no easy road to freedom . . . none of us acting alone can achieve success. We must therefore act together as a united people, for national reconciliation, for nation building, for the birth of a new world."[9]

In chapter 2 we heard from leaders in every sphere about the power of gender equality and the potential for thriving that exists if we could work together. Mutuality is the way to get there. The idea that women are better than men is as oppressive as patriarchy. Mutuality is the way to unlock the potential of gender equity in a way that benefits everyone. Our difference is our strength if we will choose to identify and use it together. Our perspectives, backgrounds, cultures, gifts, and experiences are different. And we could lead with the benefit of more information, felt realities, and gifts. This will benefit our leadership and yield transformational results.

Our best hope at transforming this world into a better one is through mutuality. Men and women don't just "complete" each other—we increase each other's capacities. We become more as we celebrate our differences and practice mutuality. When we understand our difference as essential to our shared humanity, we will come to understand that we need each other to be the best we can be. Even hearing the words *we need each other* can have a powerful healing effect. Seth Richardson said, "The restoration of our sexuality and the healing of gender dynamics does not come by fear and avoidance, by multiplying shame or guilt. We really were meant to flourish together and need each other to cultivate love, respect, and mutuality."[10]

DIFFERENCE

MUTUALITY

A growing example of how difference and mutuality can be held together for good is the renewed interest in personality types. If you don't know your Enneagram number these days, you can get very lost in the present cultural conversation. But the Enneagram, and tools like it, are a great means of embracing our differences while at the same time understanding our mutuality (our need for one another). Many have found this strategy useful for breaking down gender bias for decisions and roles. When you are in a mixed crowd, consider using a personality test to emphasize difference and grouping people together by learning types rather than gender.

Anywhere and anytime we can rediscover the value of our differences, we confront the fear that keeps us from thriving. Far from needing to be afraid of difference, we can celebrate and explore how we become better together through mutuality.

Things to Think About

- Is fear dominating decisions you are currently making or not making?
- How has fear distorted your perception in the past?
- In what ways have you confronted fear before?
- Can you think of how women or men could add value because of their differences?

SIX

How We Live

The Pull Back of Segregation, the Push Forward of Proximity

> I define connection as the energy that exists between people when they feel seen, heard, and valued; when they can give and receive without judgment; and when they derive sustenance and strength from the relationship.
>
> —BRENÉ BROWN

I once had a traumatic experience with a very big spider. I was visiting my friends Doug and Karen Hammond, missionaries in a remote village nestled into the majestic hills of KwaZulu-Natal. One evening we were swapping stories and having a great time together. Before long it was time for me to go back to my room across a field, a stone's throw away from their house. I arrived without much of a fuss but totally froze when I opened the door to my room. In front of me, on the wall, was the biggest spider I had ever seen. I already had a strong dislike for spiders—what I considered to be a healthy fear—but this thing was massive! It was larger than my whole hand! I didn't know what to do, but I did know what I couldn't do—I could not enter that room. I quickly closed the door and ran back across the field to my friend's house.

Though I knew I'd never hear the end of it, my terror helped me summon the courage I needed to knock on the door and explain my situation. Sure enough, my friend had a good laugh, but he did follow me back to my place to help me.

When we opened the door, he saw the sheer size of the truly monstrous spider and immediately stopped laughing. His eyes wide with terror, he closed the door and announced, "That's the biggest spider I have ever seen *in my whole life!*" Keep in mind he had lived in Africa for more than a few years.

Not sure what to do, he resorted to the lamest plan of attack in the history of attack plans. He pulled off one of his shoes, opened the door, and, as fast as he could, launched his shoe like a missile toward the gigantic spider. The only problem was that he missed! We both watched in horror as the spider scurried away, now hidden somewhere in *my room*. My friend shrugged his shoulders, smiled, and said, "Well, I tried!"

I couldn't believe it. I wanted *out* of that room for forever! The problem was that it was the only place for me to stay. Everything in me screamed that I needed to escape sleeping in the same room as the terrifying spider, but I had no other choice. I had to stay there. Needless to say, I did not sleep. Instead, I stayed up, readying myself to face my fear—this time with my own shoe, and at a much closer proximity. What I learned, though, is helpful. It is a completely natural impulse to want to put distance between yourself and the things you are afraid of.

In our current scenario I believe the spider is the hidden presence of terrifying things—like sexual abuse. And when there is a conversation about men and women working together, it's as if a big spider is lying in wait, ready to pounce.

In truth, many people find themselves wanting to create as much space as possible between themselves and even the thought of gender reconciliation. At its core it's about fear and self-protection. But the stark reality is that this approach fuels the problem. How will we ever rid the room of its spider when we simply shut the door and carry on with life as usual? Someone has to stick around and deal with what lurks in the dark corners of the room. In other words, solutions come from proximity.

In contrast, many people act as if the easiest solution to the difficulties of women and men working together is segregation, though they wouldn't necessarily call it that. Women end up establishing and running things for women. And men stick to men. I'm convinced this is based on a primal fear.

We're at a pivotal moment. It's time we face our fears.

Sheryl Sandberg, from her research at Lean In, put it like this: "In the wake of the #MeToo movement, it's clearer than ever we need to put an end to sexual harassment. . . . But that's not enough. . . . There's evidence of a backlash that could be harmful to women: twice as many male managers now feel uncomfortable working alone with a woman. This is a huge step in the wrong direction. More than ever, we need men working with—and mentoring—women."[1] When more women lead, workplaces are stronger and safer for everyone.

Recently I launched Women Speakers Collective, a movement to identify, train, and launch female speakers onto main stages. I know many women who speak only to women, not because they feel particularly called or gifted to, but because there is no other option. They aren't invited or welcomed or sought after for mixed or male audiences. Based on a quick count of the conferences and gatherings that are designed and led by men, one might even deduce that much of mainstream Christian culture is segregated. Because I do a lot of speaking to mixed audiences, and I have often led in places often reserved for men, I have had some delightful experiences seeing men and women being better together. I didn't set out to accomplish that. I just bulldozed my way through using grit, gift, and ignorance. Many women ask me how I did it. And for most of my life I didn't even realize I was doing anything. What I did sense was a lack of other women doing it. When I started to look around for clues, I realized that many of the most powerful female communicators I knew were speaking to women. They would occasionally get invited to a mixed or male event, but for the most part the best way (and often only way) to work on their communications skills was to female audiences. As much as I love women and know that there is a time and place for unique messages intended for separate audiences, on the whole, gender segregation is not helping us.

Segregation as a Strategy

When I even mention the word *segregation*, no doubt you will think of the civil rights movement in America. In the southern states particularly, the issue of segregation and integration was and is still a big one. Some people believed it was a good idea to separate people on the basis of color. They assigned places to live, schools, restaurants, and public places to people based on the color of their skin. Even now we are discovering neighborhoods virtually segregated until recently because of real-estate practices that refused to sell homes to people of color in neighborhoods across America. We call that systemic racism. It is profoundly wrong. But separating people because of difference is not just an American problem.

South Africa established an entire government on the idea. The National Party (Afrikaan) took power after the 1948 general election and began to implement a program of apartheid—the legal system of political, economic, and social separation of the races intended to maintain and extend political and economic control of South Africa by the white minority. Segregation was about taking control through isolation and systemic oppression.

Even a country like Canada, known for its strong commitment to egalitarianism in recent days, practiced segregation (and some would argue still practices segregation) in its treatment of First Nations people (original inhabitants of the land) through a reservation system. For almost sixty years (since 1885), the government of Canada enforced a system that required a pass for First Nations people in western provinces to even leave their reserves.[2]

We could cite many examples, as human history is rife with the failure of segregation. The fear-based response to tension around difference is rooted in a wound and never leads to anything good. And yet we persist.

Even now we are moving dangerously quickly toward a world where the reality of segregation between women and men working together is seen *as an option*. At first it presents itself as a quick solution to a pressing problem, but in reality, it only increases oppression. Clearly, separating people based on a difference they cannot control has never led to anything helpful. May our past provide us with a warning—moving toward segregation as an answer to our fear of difference will only increase division and lead to ever-increasing cycles of oppression.

On a transformational visit to South Africa, I desperately tried to understand how that country emerged from apartheid without a civil war. I immersed myself in the narrative. I read everything I could find that Mandela wrote. I studied the Truth and Reconciliation Commission, which sought to bring all people together to seek the truth in hopes of reconciliation and forgiveness as a way forward. I visited Robben Island and lay on the prison bunk that was Mandela's home for decades. I visited the District Six Museum and heard the story of oppression. I was also scheduled to visit a church that was "white." It wasn't technically or officially a "white" church because that was now illegal. But in practice it was. The community was still segregated by economics. "The church reflects the community, which is still predominantly white" is what they told me. Except that wasn't exactly true.

One of the injustices of apartheid was that the government

forced people from rural towns into work camps that became "townships." Not only did this segregate people according to color, it also separated families, destroying the fabric of rural life. I had recently visited a thriving ministry in a township a few miles away from where I was now staying for the night.

When I arrived at the pastor's house, I was a learning sponge. Now was my opportunity to hear about the transition out of apartheid from a new perspective. I started asking questions. But this time, the response was unnerving. I asked about the difficulty of the transition, and they responded that there had been no difficulty. I questioned their response, thinking they were just being nice. Surely a major shift in the political structure of their country had left them a little shaken? A little changed? They assured me that their everyday reality had not changed. Not even a little bit.

I asked if they had done anything to start reaching out to the township that was a few miles away from their church—the one I had just visited, witnessing an amazing ministry. They told me they didn't ever go "that way." I was shocked. I couldn't believe it. They lived a few miles away from one of the most segregated, isolated, oppressive systems of apartheid, and they had never even been to visit! I asked if they weren't even curious about how people lived? Perhaps they wondered about the people who were trapped in the systemic realities of segregation? They didn't see how it related to their lives or their ministry. I didn't know what to say.

It became painfully obvious that segregation creates distance, and distance can feel better than tension. The trouble is that we can go on with our lives as though nothing has changed, thinking we are saving ourselves from the pain of changing things.

But then nothing will actually change. Segregation and distance establish the status quo. They perpetuate the inevitability of inequality. They refuse a face-to-face with the people behind the oppression. And that is oppression.

Exchanging Segregation for Proximity

It's incredibly easy to judge the people I met that day, but for a moment let's put ourselves in their place. After all, a lot had changed in their country. If they were to go to the township, what would they say? How would they feel if they acknowledged the luxury and freedom of their lives compared to the pain and suffering of those stuck inside the gates? That might turn up the volume of their guilt and their complicity in the oppressive system of apartheid. How could you move forward without making sweeping changes to your own life? This is the cost of proximity. Proximity is a confrontation. That's why so many people choose not to face it.

In this context, nothing changes without proximity. One mile away might as well be one million.

The apartheid government is an extreme example of segregation. But some form of segregation exists in every oppression. Female leaders are often faced with separation from male leaders. Women find themselves regularly isolated and left out of decision-making conversations. I know of many female leaders who have been asked to leave gatherings because of their gender. Many more who, even though they are technically allowed, won't go to male-dominated events, especially leadership ones, because they feel unwelcome. This is a form of virtual segregation and it's oppressive.

The option is ours. We can either pretend like it isn't a problem. Like it never affects us. Like we don't care. We can be afraid to get closer, refuse to really take a good and honest look at the issues we're facing, and ignore the people behind them. Or we can make our way one mile in the right direction. We can move toward each other. We can get involved. Our tendencies to resist, to ignore, to isolate, and to segregate are strong and natural responses to fear.

Proximity is part of the solution. The closer we are to one another, the more realistic and possible a shared future becomes. We break strongholds by choosing to move toward each other. We break biases by seeing for ourselves. Without proximity there is no impact. You can hold all the opinions you want on gender equality, but if you don't have an integrated leadership team, you will not be part of transforming the future.

With all of these examples of racial segregation, I'm sure you must be asking yourself what systemic racism has to do with gender. Prejudice is a crossroad of sexism and racism. These oppressions are entwined at many of the same intersections of history. They are in effect the same prejudice. Gender and race are two wings on the same bird. And the response is often the same. Segregation.

Seeing Each Other

We need proximity to move toward the solution, but it's challenging because we are afraid of each other. The only answer to what we don't know is in choosing to know—to face our fears. And if you want the answers, you'll have to get closer to the people left out of the conversation. Segregation is ultimately deeply connected to how we see each other. We can hold prejudices and misconceptions for a long time if we are distanced from each other. One of the great ways we confront our prejudices and misconceptions is through inclusion. Getting close to each other will enable us to really know each other. That knowledge will lead to change.

Recently I was involved in a series of podcasts with The Meeting House church entitled "Her Story."[3] It is a five-part exploration on women, the Scriptures, and the church. The senior pastor, Bruxy Cavey, did the final preach in the series and responded to several questions people sent in. One of them was about segregated accountability groups. The person who asked the question was suggesting that there are times, especially in personal accountability, where it makes total sense to keep women and men in segregated groups. They specifically cited the moral purity conversations around pornography or sexual behavior.

As I heard the question, I thought it wasn't a bad exception to the rule; maybe there are times when segregated ministry is a helpful experience. But Bruxy had another idea. Doing the research for the series had made him question the wisdom of segregating accountability to gender-based groups. He wondered aloud if consistently talking about our moral failures or addictions to sexual, exploitative behaviors in the absence of the people who are affected by those failures and behaviors might be part of the problem with the lack of freedom from those very behaviors!

As he talked, I had a deeper revelation of the power behind

this thinking. Again, it's the power of proximity. Imagine if you had to express your regret, remorse, and repentance of exploitative behavior to the people who were most affected by it! It's both terrifying and convicting. It might deeply impact a man who struggles with pornography if he were to hear from a woman who has been wounded by it. Isn't trying to get free from objectifying other people by refusing to let them be part of the conversation possibly fueling more objectifying behavior? I'm not suggesting that this is the only way to freedom—I'm just suggesting we think about it differently. How entrenched have we become to segregated solutions? As I contemplated this strategy, I was reminded of the powerful impact of restorative justice circles. When someone has committed a crime, traditionally that person is caught, tried, and put into prison. It feels like the problem is sorted out because the guilty person is punished. The reality is that the rates of recidivism are high (the average around 50 percent).[4] Just because someone is punished, it doesn't mean that person will change the behavior. Restorative justice strategies offer ways of getting to the deeper areas of broken relationships. If the offender has admitted guilt and is willing to assume responsibility, the offender is given the opportunity to meet with the victim and/ or those who suffered because of the crime. This meeting is a confrontation that leads to repairing the harm, but even more than that, it gets to the deeper roots of broken relationships. The reported rate of recidivism after participation in restorative justice strategies is much lower (2 to 8 percent) than the prison average.[5] Those are some pretty significant statistics.

Proximity is always the best path to healing, though not the easiest way. Segregation is easy. But the best way? The way that holds the most possibility for our freedom together? That's proximity.

It's time to resist the urge to separate. Instead let's take the time, make the space, and expend the energy to draw closer to each other.

Things to Think About

- Where have you witnessed gender segregation?
- Are you afraid of women? Are you afraid of men? Why?
- How would you feel if you were the one "not allowed" in a meeting / leadership team / mentoring group based on something you couldn't control or change?
- Have you witnessed some of the joys of proximity?
- How can you use inclusion as a strategy toward understanding and relationship?

SEVEN

How We See

The Pull Back of Patriarchy,
the Push Forward of Clarity

It isn't that they can't see the solution. It is that they can't see the problem.

—G. K. CHESTERTON

read an article recently that stated Wall Street leaders were using an "avoid women at all costs" memo to deal with the #MeToo movement and its implication.[1] It seemed a little harsh. Although we can identify with the fear that the movement has unearthed, the reality is that they are not alone in this knee-jerk reaction to the difficulty of equity and accountability.

In the previous chapter we learned that in wanting an instant solution, our immediate response is to distance ourselves from the problem. In the current wave of today's issues, we think the "problem" is women. This is a fascinating reaction to the exposure of the actual problem of men behaving badly. Why would the answer to men treating women badly be to ban women from men? That makes no sense. If the actual problem is men treating women badly, then the remedy to that problem would be to ban men from the workplace. Why do we keep rehashing the idea that women are the problem? This is where we head a little deeper into the prejudice behind gender inequity.

The Blurred Lens of Patriarchy

Viewing women as the "problem" or the "temptress" or "seductive" is a genuine feature of patriarchy that goes back a very long way. It's a cultural bias inherited from thousands of years of attitudes, thoughts, actions, books, films, stories, and social norms. A bias is when you are not able to see the facts without prejudice. And a prejudice is when you already hold an opinion about a social construct. Your prejudice will *always* distort your perception. So things like segregation will always look like a good idea if you have a prejudice that women are the problem.

The opportunity we have in this cultural moment is to challenge those assumptions, name our prejudices, and then change them. But the temptation, because of the work it will require of us, is to slide into an easy and old pattern of denial, blame, and avoidance.

You may be thinking that Wall Street has its issues and shouldn't be used as an example of leadership. But let's talk about our Christian version of this gender-based bias. It's what is commonly known as the Billy Graham Rule.

Billy Graham is one of my evangelical heroes. When he was starting out in itinerant ministry, he made a list of guidelines that included governance of his finances, accountability of his power, and how he approached relationships with other women besides his wife. He was emerging at a time in the United States when his peers were besieged by sex, money, and power. He watched them crashing and burning and felt prompted to put some fences in his life to guard him from falling into those same ditches. In 1948, he made a rule for himself to not "travel, meet, or eat alone with a woman other than [his] wife."[2] This was designed to help protect him in his itinerant life. Keep in mind that in that year women in America couldn't serve on a jury, run a marathon, get a credit card, go to a coed Ivy League school, keep their job if they were pregnant, practice law, refuse sex with their husbands, or speak up about sexual harassment.[3]

To create safe boundaries for your life and ministry is a good idea. But taking the ones created for a specific set of circumstances at a certain point in time for a specific person and applying them to your life and ministry *today* is unhelpful, and in today's world, actually harmful to women. Consider for a moment that you also decided to adjust your income to the annual salary Billy Graham took in 1948—you would be making $15,000 a year. No doubt you would balk at taking a salary set in 1948 and applying it to today's average salaries, and you would be right. Why would we consider it appropriate to do the exact same thing with boundaries that end up excluding women from leadership?

I was speaking at a church and could not figure out why, even though I was staying at a hotel only five minutes from the campus, they insisted I take an Uber back and forth. I don't mind taking Ubers. I quite enjoy it. But it seemed a little bit unnecessary.

When the Uber pulled up at the church, the senior pastor met me at the door, and we continued on. I wondered why he couldn't have just picked me up on his way. That's when my assistant helped fill in the blanks. The leaders of this church were all men, and having a female speaker meant that none of them could pick me up and be alone with me in a car for the five-minute drive to the church. The whole situation made me feel weird. Plus, my Uber driver was male, and it didn't seem to bother him! What was the point of that restriction? Were they worried that I couldn't control myself or that they couldn't? Or that people would honestly think on the five-minute drive to the church at eight in the morning, after having just met, we were going to have an affair? The reason I'm sharing the experience is it just happened. But it all started in 1948. Prejudice distorts our perception. Our theology, culture, and church can prevent us from seeing women as leaders.

It's important to know that we are living in a context that invites us to view each other differently.

Most of you will balk at the idea of slavery or even racism or sexism or anything that would limit people's callings or convictions or giftings. But your ideals are not the only problem. The way things are constructed is the problem. This is *systemic sexism*. Women are excluded because of the way the system and structure are *designed*.

I'm not sure what Billy Graham thought of women leaders. I know all the women in his life say that he was a beautiful and supportive influence. He was good. And good to them. The problem isn't Graham—it's the system, structure, and attitudes of his culture and, even more problematic, his subculture, which kept women excluded and segregated from main structures and opportunities.

The Billy Graham Rule was established to protect men, not to protect women. And that's more to the point. Protecting male leaders meant isolating and vilifying women. I don't think anyone *intended* that. It's just what happens when you create systems based on the idea that women are the "enemy" or the "temptress" or the thing from which you need to protect yourself.

The Jesus Rule

Jesus didn't keep the Billy Graham Rule. And his culture was *way* more infused with patriarchy than Graham's was. Jewish leaders in Jesus' day used to wake up thanking God in a daily prayer that they weren't born a woman. To allow a woman to train as a disciple was outrageous. To be alone with a woman was absolutely out of the question. Yet Jesus encouraged female discipleship and was alone with a woman. He was able to see things and people a different way. He didn't see women through the blurred lens of patriarchy. He didn't see women as a threat. He didn't see women as a liability. He didn't even see women as a temptation to resist. He saw women as sacred, as leaders, as blessed. He saw women as people. He had a clear view of reality.

Women are no longer culturally or subculturally (we hope) servants of men. The culture has changed and shifted, and the church has begun to catch up to the ways and will of Jesus in our practices. Women have developed their gifting and leadership capacity and are ready and willing to serve as leaders in every area. But they are not seen that way. And this is a problem. The way we view each other needs to change.

Often, even churches who believe women can and should lead can't seem to identify female leaders among themselves. Sometimes the effects of segregating the sexes in ministry have made us blind to each other. Male leaders don't often have the occasion to see women using their gifts, and because they hold the power, they are unable to see women as leaders.

Consider this confession by a male leader: "As a male, I benefit from patriarchy-infected structures, which means I'm often blind to the insidious effects. I need to continually hear from my sisters how and when they feel ignored and overlooked."[4]

And women don't often recognize their natural talent or leadership potential. Cultural clues and social norms insist they get in line with the status quo. Many gifted female leaders remain unidentified in systems all over the world. The way we view each other needs to change. Our distorted or limited perspective perpetuates exclusion through a vast array of structures/systems/attitudes/prejudices that bar women from leadership.

So let's change them. We can change them by embracing the truth, imagining the possibilities, and confronting the barriers. We need to trade our patriarchal glasses for some clearer lenses.

Clearing the Lens

Trying to clean that lens is a challenge. But it's an important work in clarifying and clearing up the implications of the gender divide.

There is an interesting little video that breaks down Hollywood's portrayal of women in their films using what they call the Hollywood Rule or the Bechdel Test. To pass the test as a movie that presents women as active humans instead of passive objects, they created these criteria: The movie has to have at least two women characters. Those characters need to have names. And they have to talk to each other (even just one time) about anything other than a man. That's it. Two women. With names. A conversation between them about anything other than a man. As of 2015, do you know how many movies passed the test? A handful. Think of all of your favorite movies and apply the test. This is what we mean by a patriarchal lens. Patriarchy is a view of the world that has been constructed through a male-dominated culture.

Why not create a similar test for your work or community? How about your church culture? Are there more than two women leaders on your stage whose names you know? Are there more than two female speakers you can name? Are there two or more executives in your leadership that have female names? Do they interact with each other around things other than a man? Have you read two theological books by women? Can you name them? Are there two women athletes you are inspired by? You get the idea.

I've found this test to be a very helpful revelation of the blurred lens of patriarchy that exists in our communities and, ultimately, a way to begin changing the way we see.

Another way to clear up the way we see each other is when things get personal. I think that as our culture has shifted, we have had more proximity to women as complex, gifted, capable leaders. The closer you are to someone, the clearer your vision of that person becomes. The concept of empowerment and inclusion and mutuality and opportunity has moved from a "good idea" and even a "theologically inspired" one to a personal one. This has changed the way we are viewing each other! I've had conversations with very successful male leaders who are now extremely interested in equity because their daughters have leadership gifts and they finally feel the reality of gender limitations in existing structures and systems. Because they see their daughters clearly, they also start to see the obstacles. When things get personal, they get closer and our perspective shifts. Far from talking about the theory of empowerment, the conversation moves toward a felt need to change for the sake of our daughters and sons. It's an important shift.

I had a founder of a church-planting movement speak to me about this recently. Convinced that recruiting and training women church planters is part of the solution to advancing the church, he was struggling to find women to become church planters. How could we get more women into church planting? We quickly realized that in many denominations women don't even know they *can* church plant. In many other churches the entire leadership team of the church is male, so women rightly deduce that even if they were to lead a church plant, it would be extremely difficult if not impossible to do.

There are also very few examples of current church plants led by women. It started to dawn on all of us that women will never identify as church planters if they never view themselves as church planters. And men will never identify women as church planters if they can't see women that way. It's not just a structural issue; it's a perspective problem. Women viewed through the lens of patriarchy are not seen as they are, and as a result of a distorted vision, their potential is never realized.

In the business world we talk about hitting walls, but in gender equity it's traditionally been called a glass ceiling—a real and present but invisible barrier for women (and minorities) to enter leadership or governance inside structures or systems dominated by males in power. It's often when you start to research or take some steps toward achieving gender equity that you discover it in your own business, church, or community. It's an invisible barrier, so it is very difficult to name and fight. Usually more than a rule or a line or even a boundary, it's rooted in practices, systems, and cultural norms that limit women from entering, participating, and growing into the leaders they are meant to be.

The challenge is rooted in how we see the world. The lenses we have seen through have been shaped by our cultural realities and have shaped a mind-set that keeps us blind to the things we need to change the most. We need a way to clear our perspective, and one way to change the way we see is by changing the way we think. We can shift our vision by changing our minds.

Things to Think About

- Do we view women as a threat? With suspicion? Do we objectify women as sexual temptations?
- Are there women with leadership gifts in your community? How would you discover them?
- If you are male, do you feel like you need to protect women from you? Why?
- What do you need to change in your community that would help everyone see each other more clearly?
- What is the truth about how women are viewed and treated? Are women at your leadership table? Why not?

EIGHT

How We Think

The Pull Back of Rooted Beliefs, the Push Forward of Transformed Beliefs

My greatest challenge has been to change the
mind-set of people.

—MUHAMMAD YUNUS

Our mind-set—what we believe and how we think—influences what we do. Shifting a mind-set is a deeply difficult process, but it also holds the most transformational opportunity for change. Without a mind-set shift, you may change structures, systems, and institutions, but those changes rarely last. What we believe is at the root of everything we do.

Ellen Duffield in her book, *Brave Women*, explained the

phenomenon of women's career development and the close link between a woman's self-perceived ability and her professional success. "While sixty-nine percent of young girls (the same percentage as boys) consider themselves leaders, only thirty-six percent are interested in being a leader when they get older. There is also a strong correlation between the beliefs we have in our own ability and how well we will perform a task or range of actions."[1] People with strong confidence take more risks and persevere through obstacles they encounter.

Remember that transformational trip to Rwanda? I asked World Relief how they were experiencing such remarkable changes as they worked with the government of Rwanda to rebuild the nation after the devastation of the genocide. The country is achieving significant success in its own transformation. How did they get such transformation at regional and national levels? They told me about the mind-set-shift training and its amazing results.

Eager to discover more about the way transformation was happening in rural villages and regional networks, I sat in with a group of pastors (called a church empowerment zone) who shared about how their lives and ministries and communities have been transformed. Again, they said it began with the mind-set-shift training. They had individual testimonies and community impacts to report.

One pastor said he used to beat his wife. He thought that was what you should do to "be a man." It was what his father had done and many other mentors in his life. But during the mind-set training he realized that his belief system was misguided. At the root of his behavior was fear. He thought if he was soft or caring or relational with his wife, she wouldn't respect him and would leave. He was able to identify not just the problematic behavior but the root of that behavior. He was afraid of being alone. Once he identified the root of the behavior, he could change his belief. He came to understand that if he didn't want his wife to leave him, he should talk to her, include her in decisions, be kind to her. Once he had that light-bulb moment, both in identifying the root of his behavior and some solutions to it, he acted on it. He said he never realized a marriage could be so fulfilling or a relationship could be so life giving.

He naturally shared his story with some other people, and soon many couples found their way to this man's house for mind-set-shift training that would transform their marriages as well. Marriage by marriage, the community began to see transformation in relationships and behaviors. Through this training alone, World Relief's most recent impact report stated that there was a 60 percent reduction in the acceptance of domestic violence. Health, economics, child development, and nutrition also saw dramatic changes in positive outcomes.[2]

A Rooted Belief System

Rwanda's mind-set-shift training uses the simple illustration of a tree. Luke 6:43 is their inspiration. It's where Jesus told us that if the fruit is bad, then the problem is not just with the fruit—it's with the tree. They explain that the root system of a tree is underground but is essential to the health of the tree.

Likening the roots to our beliefs, they explain that what you believe is underneath everything you do in life. What you believe will influence what you value. Your values are the trunk of your tree. Your values are what give you the ability to act. Like the branches of a tree, your actions are ways you express your values in everyday life. And your actions are what determine the fruit your life produces. The fruit is the result of action, springing from values, informed by beliefs. So if you don't like the results of your life, you cannot just pick off the fruit and call it a day. You must look at your actions, which will reveal your values and expose your false beliefs. Changing the quality of your life's output requires planting true beliefs that will grow better fruit. In short, you need to trace the results of your life to the root system in your heart.

I heard many stories from people who were scared to let needy people into their lives for fear of being taken advantage of. I heard poor people who were afraid of being tricked or used by the church. But all of them began the process of uncovering the root of their isolating, violent, and fear-based beliefs that led them to damaging behaviors. Once they identified those roots, they traced the connection of their behaviors to their beliefs.

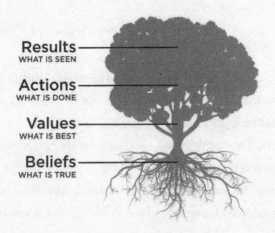

Results — WHAT IS SEEN

Actions — WHAT IS DONE

Values — WHAT IS BEST

Beliefs — WHAT IS TRUE

The mind-set shift is a simple and effective tool. It almost seems too easy to be true. But I listened to countless stories and saw the transformation myself. Could it really be that simple?

I think mind-set shifts are a very effective way of connecting the dots in our gender-equity discussion. What we believe will influence what we value, which will lead to what we do, which will be visible through results. What we are seeing in this #MeToo era is a lot of bad fruit. Abuse, harassment, inequity, seclusion, disempowerment, and many other types of "rotten apples" that have grown from damaged root systems. The temptation is to just remove the bad fruit as fast as possible and think the job is done. Maybe we can prosecute the leaders who were called out for their bad behavior—just a few bad apples in a barrel of good ones. It's what we want to do. We want to scapegoat the problem because we long for the problem to be outside of us.

But if our churches, families, relationships, systems, and structures are bearing this kind of fruit, we cannot fail to trace that behavior to the root. If we want real change, not just short-term reactions, we need a massive mind-set shift when it comes to gender relationships. Because what we believe affects what we do. So although you may not be abusive toward women, if your leadership team or culture doesn't include women, doesn't treat women as contributors and cocreators, and doesn't create space for them to be part of leadership, it might be exposing your *real* beliefs.

Research has shown us that gender biases are inherent in systems and human decisions. Because we are susceptible to unconscious stereotypes and social pressure to conform to deeply embedded social behaviors, we need an "abrupt external shock" to interrupt business as usual![3]

What you are looking at when you see a lack of equity in your own sphere of influence is fruit from the tree that is your belief system. You have to ask yourself why. I think many of us would like to say it's not what we believe. We value women. But to say you value women and then continue to not identify, invest in, or develop potential women leaders uncovers rooted beliefs.

We have to uproot and replant our root system if we are going to change.

A Critical Shift in Mind-Set

I've been captivated with the life of Malala Yousafzai. Part of my fascination is that such an incredibly strong young woman came from a culture that doesn't always celebrate girls. Malala started standing up for the right of girls to go to school when she was just a girl herself. At age fifteen, because she refused to stop speaking out, the Taliban shot her in the head. Miraculously she survived and went on to become an international ambassador for girls' education through the UN. A reporter once asked her how she did it. How did she become Malala the girl activist from Pakistan?

She said it began with her father. She explained that in her culture when a baby boy is born, the family comes to celebrate. They all bring money and throw it in the crib and speak out a blessing, "This baby is a gift from God." But when girls are born, no money is brought and no blessing spoken. Malala said that her father, even though he wasn't wealthy, began to save money for her birth. When the family arrived, he gave out his money and told them all to throw it in the crib because Malala was a blessing from God. Malala grew up with that belief system.[4] Because she believed that, she has consistently borne fruit in keeping with that belief. She has been a blessing to the world! What if all of us had that kind of mind-set about each other? What would it mean for us to defy our cultural prejudices and celebrate the diversity woven into the fabric of our children? It could change everything.

Ellen Duffield has spent decades researching leadership and what keeps women from thriving. Explaining her quest, she talked about the compulsion she felt as she observed strong, talented women lacking self-confidence to change the world. She wrote, "I discovered that girls aged 6 already believe boys are more likely to be 'really, really smart' than girls, and that a woman's confidence peaks at age 9! I discovered that low self esteem is linked to lower academic scores, higher mental health issues, an increase in negative behaviours and corresponding decrease in participation in various positive activities."[5]

For both men and women, it's imperative to find the connection between our belief systems and change. The effect of a mind-set shift is powerful. Believing that women are a true gift of God and understanding them as equal, vital, gifted, and contributors to the world will not only change your behavior—it will also change theirs! Because Malala's father believed she was a gift, she believed that about herself and acted accordingly. The reality of a mind-set shift is crucial for women. Women often have a distorted belief system about themselves that has been shaped under the soil of our culture for their entire lives.

The research clearly shows us that we are creating a generation of girls whose self-confidence is in desperate need of rebuilding. From an early age, "their confidence starts to fade, slipping away as insecurities, doubts, and body image issues begin to take hold. How can we reverse this troubling trend? How can we create a generation of girls whose confidence and self-esteem continues to rise throughout their teenage years, past the age of nine, propelling them into leadership roles and successful careers?"[6]

What women believe about *themselves* is ripe for a mind-set shift and is connected to how they think the rest of the world values them. If self-confidence remains one of the reasons women don't become leaders, surely it's time to change it. But how we change the way women think about themselves is deeply connected to changing the way we think about each other. We need a mind-set shift, together. It's time to change our minds so we can see each other through the sacred lens of God's world-view. After all, the image of God is embedded in each of us, and if we could believe that, we could see it. With a transformed belief at the base of our attitudes and behaviors, we can grow values and actions that bear flourishing fruit.

> Seven in 10 girls believe they are not good enough or do not measure up in some way, including their looks, performance in school, and relationships with family and friends.[7]

Things to Think About

- Do you notice that women/girls in your community are lacking in self-confidence?
- Do you encourage women to try things they may not have thought they could do?
- Do you struggle to find/identify female leaders? Why do you think that is?
- Have you been surprised at the talent in a woman who thought she didn't have what it takes?

Ideas to Implement:

- Start developing young girls for leadership early.
- Girls ages nine to eleven are at a key stage of development and need ways to fight back against the cultural norms.
- Sponsor women leaders. Many studies suggest that to break through the glass ceiling requires much more than hard work by women themselves. Women often only succeed if someone on the other side of the power structure invites a woman to the next level.
- Is there a promising woman leader you can invite to the next level?

NINE

How We Connect

The Pull Back of Porn,
the Push Forward of Truth

Our desire for truth has to outweigh our commitment to comfort.

—KEN WYTSMA

Doug struggled with a porn addiction for at least a decade of his adult life. What started as a sneak peek at tantalizing and sexually arousing material turned into a damaging, soul-destroying habit. In his recovery he spent some time unearthing the damage porn had done. His marriage was lost, his self-esteem had plummeted, and his relationships with everyone seemed to erode as his addiction led him to isolation and shame. But what struck me most forcefully was how Doug had become so afraid of women. He was afraid of sex. He was afraid of intimacy. So much had been lost. Doug's story is not new or even unique. In our current culture, sex has been distorted from its original purpose.

Susie's uncle introduced her to sexual intimacy. He told her it was a gift. But it didn't feel like it. Pain and pleasure mixed in Susie's brain, causing shame and fear to lodge in her heart. She felt dirty. She tried to shake it off, but after many years of self-harm, toxic relationships, sexual addiction, and mental-health issues, she finally got help. Unraveling the toxic behavioral patterns took some time, but at the root was the sexual abuse from her childhood. The damage of abusive sexual experiences is extensive and tragic.

Sex is meant to be good. At least that's how it was created. Far from objectifying, using, harming, shaming, and distorting our differences, sex was and still can be an incredible display of people who are different enjoying each other. Sex in a healthy marriage demonstrates how difference and mutuality can lead to flourishing. Just ask any marriage counselor. Sex, in its finest form, is a way of celebrating each other, sharing power, expressing love, bearing fruit. Deborah Hirsch in her book *Redeeming Sex* reminded us that ultimately sex is designed to help us understand God. So how did it get so distorted?

To talk about sex today is often paralyzing, confusing, and alienating. Rather than demonstrating the goodness of gender unity and the ultimate eternal connection we long for, sex has become one of the greatest enemies of mutuality in the difference between genders. The National Sexual Violence Resource Center in America's most recent studies say that in the United States one in three women and one in six men have experienced some form of sexual violence in their lifetimes.[1]

We are reminded regularly of the ugly reality of sex as an appalling misuse of power and have been bearing the consequences. But those effects are not just destroying women's well-being. They are also eroding the lives of men and the fragile fabric of the relationship between us.

From childhood, women and men have been dealing with sex as a misuse of power. The most recent statistics say that "one in four girls and one in six boys will be sexually abused before they turn 18 years old."[2] We should all be completely and utterly horrified by these statistics. They bring names and faces to the reality of sexual abuse in our culture.

If we want to create a different future, we cannot afford to hide from the realities of these truths. It is time to choose to recognize the pain of women and men around the world who are suffering and have suffered the realities of inequality, injustice, and sexism on every level. It is time to tell those who are finally finding the courage and strength to tell their stories, "We hear you. Your story matters. And the truth you are telling is essential for us to understand oppression and to make the world a better place. Thank you." Too often we silence those who already bear the burden of shame, fear, and pain.

The cost of this is paid not only by the individuals who suffer from sexual abuse and violence but by all of us. How can we heal or grow or change if we refuse to confront the reality of fractured relationships because of our sexual attitudes and behaviors? This stark denial has forced people to hide their pain and suffer in silence. Instead, we can choose to create places of healing and wholeness and restoration, which is what it will look like to mend our relationships.

Damaging sexual behavior is a misuse of power. It has to be identified and addressed if we hope for any healing to occur in our connection with each other. In working relationships it's important to be up-front and honest about our hopes for creating a safe and respectful environment. It may seem a little simplistic, but I think it's worth mentioning that having a plan to deal with both the current reality of sexual harassment and preventing harassment in the future is essential. Having a known and communicated plan for unwanted sexual behavior is crucial when it comes to establishing a thriving culture for men and women working together.

Responding to the reality of sexual harassment will include a strong commitment of leadership, creating safe places to tell the truth and support victims, and ensuring just and fair practices for dealing with allegations. Necessary investigations should be fair and transparent; discipline for perpetrators and provision of counseling for victims are good practices. Even more powerful than responding is preventing sexual abuse from occurring at all. Essential to this reality are awareness and training for staff/ volunteers, clear and available policies and guidelines to follow, making it a priority to be a safe community, and regularly talking about the realities of sexual abuse in our culture. Removing the stigma and silence around sexual trauma helps to reduce its power.

The Power of Pornography

When I was thinking about the realities of the amount of sexual harassment in our culture that spurred the #MeToo movement, I started to wonder what the sources of the problem were. My mind flashed back to an occasion several years ago when I was speaking at a Christian university. I was using a live voting app to digitally poll my audience as I spoke about various things throughout the week. About two thousand young people and the entire faculty attended the morning chapels during this special week on campus.

One day, while speaking about the reality of human trafficking, I mentioned that one of the things that fueled the fastest-growing crime of sex trafficking was pornography. Pornography drives the demand for sex. Using the online polling app, I took a live survey during my talk with this question, "How often do you view porn?" The possible answers were (1) never, (2) sometimes, (3) always, and (4) can't stop.

The results were overwhelming. I literally took a step back on the platform as I watched in relative disbelief as young people voted on their mobile phones. "Always" and "can't stop" were adding up at an exponential rate. I'm not sure what was more surprising to me at the time—that so many kids were struggling with pornography addiction or that they were telling the truth about it in a chapel! Everyone was stunned. I connected the obvious dots between the sale of human beings for sex and the oppression of pornography that fuels the demand for it. And then I invited all of those struggling with pornography addiction to join us that night for a voluntary chapel where we would talk, pray, and begin to move toward freedom together.

Traditionally the night chapel was virtually empty. But that night it was packed. Hundreds of kids (mostly male) were there to start talking. One of those kids (let's call him George) sat next to me. Front row. He was a mess. He couldn't stop crying. He looked at me, and through his weeping he begged me to help him. He told me how he had been trapped in a cycle of addiction to pornography since he was twelve. He couldn't even stand the sight of himself in the mirror. He was only eighteen years old.

I think I already understood the link between human trafficking and pornography, but that day helped me understand the force of oppression that pornography puts on an entire generation of men and boys and an increasingly alarming rate of girls. Since that day I talk about pornography as an oppression much more frequently.

Whenever I speak about the oppression of pornography, people will often come and share their struggles with me. Many young women have asked if I thought it was possible to find a guy who isn't viewing pornography regularly. Girls began to tell me it was completely normal for guys to ask them to act out fantasies from porn, even though they found them degrading. Husbands began to admit that they couldn't perform sexually with their wives because of the effects pornography had on their brains and bodies, rendering them impotent to authentic, healthy sexual relationships. Recently many women and girls have been revealing their shameful secret of pornography addiction, not knowing what to do with the self-loathing that results.

You may think I'm overstating things, but consider these statistics Fight the New Drug uses to shed light on how pervasive pornography has become:

- "Porn sites receive more regular traffic than Netflix, Amazon, & Twitter combined *each month*. (HuffPost)
- "35% of all internet downloads are porn-related. (WebRoot)
- "34% of internet users have been exposed to unwanted porn via ads, pop-ups, etc. (WebRoot) . . .
- "At least 30% of all data transferred across the internet is porn-related. (HuffPost)
- "The most common female role stated in porn titles is that of women in their 20's portraying teenagers. (Jon Millward) (*In 2013, Millward conducted the largest personal research study on the Porn Industry in the U.S. He interviewed 10,000 porn performers about various aspects of the business.*)
- "Recorded child sexual exploitation (known as "child porn") is one of the fastest-growing online businesses. (IWF)
- "624,000+ child porn traders have been discovered online in the U.S.
- "Between 2005 and 2009, child porn was hosted on servers located in all 50 states. (Association of Sites Advocating Child Protection)
- "Porn is a global, estimated $97 billion industry, with about $12 billion of that coming from the U.S. (NBC News)
- "In 2018 alone, more than 5,517,000,000 hours of porn

were consumed on the world's largest porn site. (Pornhub Analytics)

- "Eleven pornography sites are among the world's top 300 most popular Internet sites. The most popular such site, at number 18, outranks the likes of eBay, MSN, and Netflix. (SimilarWeb) . . .
- "The world's largest free porn site also received over 33,500,000,000 site visits during 2018 alone. (Pornhub)"[3]

I'm not trying to scare us. I'm trying to wake us up to the forceful oppression that is behind the acts of sexual violence plaguing our relationships. And just in case you thought it was an adult problem, consider these statistics that ought to alert us to the present and future problem that pornography is to mutually thriving relationships between men and women.

- "64% of young people, ages 13–24, actively seek out pornography weekly or more often. . . .
- "A study of 14- to 19-year-olds found that females who consumed pornographic videos were at a significantly greater likelihood of being victims of sexual harassment or sexual assault.
- "A Swedish study of 18-year-old males found that frequent consumers of pornography were significantly more likely to have sold and bought sex than other boys of the same age.
- "A 2015 meta-analysis of 22 studies from seven countries found that internationally the consumption of pornography

was significantly associated with increases in verbal and physical aggression, among males and females alike.

- "A recent UK survey found that 44% of males aged 11–16 who consumed pornography reported that online pornography gave them ideas about the type of sex they wanted to try."[4]

How do we have a real conversation about the eroding relationship between women and men without talking about the scourge of pornography and its effect on us? We can't.

The work of exposing and treating the issue of pornography is paramount for this generation. It is clearly destroying the very basis for gender relationships to grow. To have any hope of genuine human equity in our current world, we must unravel the oppression of porn.

Confronting the Dominant Narrative

Think about it. How we see each other impacts how we treat each other. Objectification is the exact opposite of mutuality. And pornography objectifies people. As the organization Fight the New Drug explains on its website,

> Porn happens to be fantastic at forming new, long-lasting pathways in the brain. In fact, porn is such a ferocious competitor that hardly any other activity can compete with it, including actual sex with a real partner. That's right, porn

can actually overpower the brain's natural ability to have real sex! Why? As Dr. Norman Doidge, a researcher at Columbia University, explains, porn creates the perfect conditions and triggers the release of the right chemicals to make lasting changes in the brain.[5]

Porn changes your brain chemistry while it objectifies women. The viewers of porn are not passive; they are actively learning that women are not people but objects.

According to some studies, 68 percent of men admit to using porn at least once a week.[6] And that number is generally thought to be pretty conservative. Every time someone views pornography, that person rehearses a narrative. The narrative is predominantly about a male conquest of a female. To be sure, there is enough variety to leave you feeling sick, but the main narrative viewed through porn is of male dominance, male conquest, and female submission (usually involving violence). The most popular porn site in the world released its data report for 2017, and not only are the views getting exponentially bigger, but the viewers are getting younger. Fight the New Drug asks, "How do you think these collective hours and hours of content are shaping our society's understanding of sex? Especially consider how a recent study of adolescent porn use concluded that the major messages presented by porn are male domination, hypermasculinity, and making male sexual pleasure the top priority. Does that sound healthy to you?"[7]

This problem is not going away. The commodification and hypersexualization of our culture are toxic to male and female relationships, and we must address them if we want to be able to create a better future. Fight the New Drug is a campaign that's been identifying this oppression for several years and making solid attempts to stop it. Battling porn might be the only way to restoration.

Let's discover our way back to healthy and thriving relationships. I know this conversation can be overwhelming. But when I look into the fake and toxic world of pornography and learn that even there the dominant narrative is men abusing women, I can't help but wonder why. Why is male dominance the main story?

In a word, power.

Things to Think About

- Are you up to speed on the reality of pornography and its effects? Are the people in your community? Get informed.
- Can you be honest with people around you regarding pornography and your involvement? Can you create safe places for people to fight the secrecy and shame about porn addiction in order to heal?
- Would you (both women and men) make a personal decision to stop viewing pornography?
- Would you get help if you find it difficult or impossible to stop using pornography?
- Can you consider investing in healthy and whole relationships with others?

TEN

How We Act

The Pull Back of Power Abused, the Push Forward of Mutuality

Nearly all men [and women] can stand adversity; if you want to test a man's character, give him power.

—ABRAHAM LINCOLN

Men hold significantly more positions of power than women. This is true now and it's been true for a long time. As Allison Goldstein wrote,

Consider the following statistics: As of January 2018, women currently hold just 5.2% of CEO positions at S&P 500 companies. In 2016, women made up 20.2% of board seats of the

Fortune 500. In the legal field, women make up 45% of associates but only 22% of partners and 18% of equity partners. And in the political realm, women hold only 24.9% of seats in state legislatures. In short, most women do not hold [senior authority] at their jobs. Men do.

Of course, holding power doesn't inherently mean someone will sexually harass a subordinate. Dacher Keltner, a psychology professor at the University of California at Berkley, explains the effect of power leading to sexual harassment in this way: ". . . power makes you more impulsive. It makes you less worried about social conventions and less concerned about the effect of your actions on others." When we look at cases like Harvey Weinstein and Bill O'Reilly, this explanation makes sense. These men really didn't have to worry about the effects of their actions, because, until a critical mass of women stood up and said "no more," there were no consequences.[1]

Hanna Naima McCloskey, founder of Fearless Futures, explained how understanding the way power works is essential: "Sexual harassment happens because there's an asymmetry of power."[2]

I couldn't agree more. The realities that threaten our mutuality are based around power. And it is not impossible to imagine a shift in how power works in our lifetime. It's happened before! Consider for a moment the power of a priest named Martin Luther. Who knew one priest could be so powerful? No one.

A Shift in Power

Luther lived in an age where the church was dominant and corrupt. There was no doubt about it, but it wasn't only one priest who tried to change it. Many did. And most of those reformers were either sidelined or killed for trying to confront the corruption. The massive behemoth of the church was a power that could not be overthrown. It had everything: the dominant and authoritative voice, the Word of God, the money, and the power of the state (church and state were one). Who could change that? At that time in history it seemed no one could. But something did change. Power did shift. The Protestant Reformation happened. Martin Luther, a common priest stuck in the center of the giant cog of the church, took on the most massive power structure of the times. And changed things. But how?

The Protestant Reformation was a massive shift in power that culminated in the perfect storm of several factors: power was held by the church elite (a small group of corrupt, hierarchical authority), the church censored and interpreted information (controlling the narrative), a group of church folks reached their tipping point (Martin Luther the most famous leader of them), and the invention of the printing press. Every student examining the incredible impact the Protestant Reformation had on the pages of history will tell you that the printing press was a game changer when it came to power.

As one historian put it, "The Gutenberg printing press was responsible for some of the great revolutions in history, formed the basis for the modern market economy, and radically changed the socio-political structure of Europe."[3]

The Protestant Reformation culminated with a massive shift in the world that would create a *way* for everything to change. And no one saw the full impact of it coming. How could they?

What people could see was that the printing press was an incredible invention. It was going to change the game for literacy and information dissemination. It would advance the way people accessed knowledge. Everyone could see that it was a big deal. But the unintentional results of the Gutenberg printing press were even more impressive than its original intention. *It became a tool of revolution.* A systemic shift was coming, not only in information, but in power. How power was taken, controlled, and used was shaken and shifted and transformed through the printing press.

Now one priest with a big beef against the massive power structure of the church could not only walk up to the door of the church and nail his ninety-five reasons why (which is what he did), but he could also print copies and send them *everywhere* so that *everyone* could read them and know the truth for themselves. The church would inevitably try to collect the information back so it could change and control the narrative, but this was no longer a time when monks were writing furiously on felt parchment at the behest of the authority of the church itself—this was *printing* time. Hundreds and thousands of copies could be printed and sent, and no one could stop the information from being disseminated.

That didn't change the information; it changed the *power* of that information. The church would then go back into its power vault and do its best to control the situation, but it could not. People gained access to information they never had before. No longer did the masses need to rely on a priest to both read and interpret the Scriptures for them. They could read them for themselves and interpret them as well. This would rock the church in more ways than anyone could ever have predicted. But it would do even more than that. It would rewire the way society distributed power.

Another Power Shift

We would be wise to pay attention because power has shifted again. The issue of power and how it's used is at the heart of the way women and men relate to each other. The reason you are even reading this book is because a little hashtag became a movement. Many men and organizations tried to stuff the cat back in the bag and push all those wiggly worms of history back into the can. But it was too late. And why was it too late? Because the way power works in our current culture has shifted. And understanding that shift will help keep us from hanging on to something that no longer exists.

The shift of power that happened with the printing press was not just about information—it was about social structure and influence. We are living in another shift. And every boys'-club member who is used to male camaraderie and a solid grip on the control center of power should be feeling the rumbling beneath his feet. #TimesUp is not just an angry feminist response to a deep injustice; it's a social alarm clock. The time *is* up. The old systems of hoarded power, male leadership, unchanging systems of influence, and unchallenged practices of male behavior—the time is up. Not just because the behavior is wrong but because the social constructs of power have shifted. And despite our fear, this change in power will not be the end of the world; it will be the emergence of a better one.

I remember when the internet became a thing. I know this dates me, but it also allows me to think hard about the past and my experience and how the internet has become such a mainstream way of living and working. It's really hard to imagine what life was like before it existed. When email became the standard way to communicate, I sent requests to my boss at the time (who was much older than me). He would have his secretary print out the email and write his response on the bottom and have her fax it back to me! To be fair, that lovely (albeit dinosaur) of a boss was trying to adapt to a *massive transition*.

To say it was revolutionary is to understate it. The internet changed how everyone related to everything and everyone. The internet began to shake systems and structures in ways we were not prepared for. Micha Kaufman compared the Internet Revolution to the Industrial Revolution in a *Forbes* article: "The Internet Revolution IS in fact the Industrial Revolution of our time. It's a sweeping social disruption that brings with it not only new inventions and scientific advances, but perhaps most importantly revolutionizes both the methods of work and we the workers ourselves."[4]

Those who don't pay attention to this massive shift of power will only lose more of it. As Carl H. Builder wrote: "The losers of power in this change are hierarchical organizational structures everywhere which have historically been erected and sustained on the control of limited information. The effect of the change is analogous to the Renaissance, when the clerical hierarchies lost their control of information to new secular enterprises. This time, however, the diffusion of power is much more widespread; and the drama of the next few decades is how power will accrete in the new electronic networks that are rapidly shrinking the globe."[5]

I remember talking to the head of IT at a large corporation. He was trying to rein in some social media posts because they were ahead of the company. There was nothing wrong with the content; it was just that the IT department had not caught up with the necessary ways of "controlling" the information and how it was disseminated, who was reading it, and how it could be "approved." I asked him a lot of questions, the most essential one being, "Does your job feel like trying to shovel water in the middle of a rushing river?" His job was to do the exact opposite of what the internet was created for.

In a moment of transparency, he just slowly nodded his head. The old ways of the company were a disintegrating system of management that could not stand up to the new information age of the internet. As hard as you might try to apply old system standards to a new system, it will not work. You can rage against it, or you can adapt and learn how to use the new system for the best possible good. The most powerful thing about the internet is not that it gives power but that it releases people to discover the power they already have. At the heart of the sexual harassment/ abuse issue is a question about power itself. What is power? And even better, what's it for? Power is personal. We all have it. And we can all use it.

Identify Our Power

Recognizing the power we do have is an essential part of using it well. Many people are afraid to have this conversation because so much about power and privilege has been painful. If we are going to adjust our lives to fit the new social constructs of power, we have got to do the work of identifying our own. How will we ever change something we are not recognizing or acknowledging? What kind of power/privilege do we have?

I've found this model from the Canadian Council for Refugees to be a helpful tool in identifying power and privilege. It's a wheel. At the center of the wheel is the heart of power. These are the cultural norms used in a North American / Western power base that identify how close you are to the center of power.

Now, there are many different privilege wheels to choose from in a quick search on Google! The point is not to get lost on the exact wording or even values associated with the power wheel (don't overcomplicate the categories). It's a simple measurement tool for your own reflection and conversation. Ideally this is a tool that will help us get honest in our assessment of our own power.

When it comes to big, sweeping changes in culture, most of our conversations center around the power we've lost or the power we wish we had. But let's think about the power we do have for a minute.

I was using this power-wheel exercise in a room full of leaders and had a fascinating discussion. When I asked for feedback, two people responded immediately. One of them was a woman in her forties who had been doing youth work for a long time.

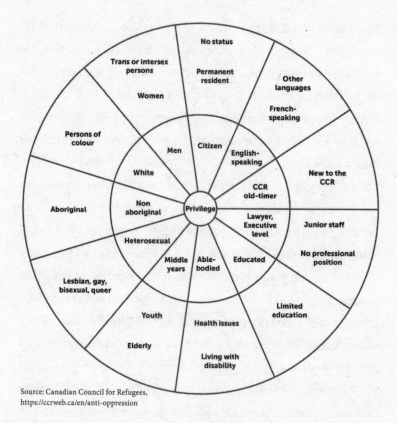

Source: Canadian Council for Refugees,
https://ccrweb.ca/en/anti-oppression

She said doing the exercise had surprised her. She had always been told that because she was a woman, she lacked power, and she believed it. But as she was filling in the wheel, she realized it wasn't true. She was genuinely surprised by the power she *did* have. As she was talking, I noticed that a gentleman in the front row was crying. It was an intense reaction, and I was wondering what he was thinking and feeling that made his response so emotive. He told me through tears that he felt a lot of shame and guilt because as he was filling in the wheel, he realized that he had all the power. He was ashamed of his power. That was fascinating and disturbing to me. "Why are you ashamed of having power?" I asked. He said he was ashamed because he thought having power meant that someone else didn't. Which raises this important question: Is it wrong to have power? Is it wrong to inherit status? Is power negative? These are important questions because ultimately what we think about power will influence how we use it.

Let's begin with this. How do you use the power you have?

Power is the capacity or ability to direct or influence the behavior of others or the course of events. Abuse is to use something (or someone) to bad effect or for a bad purpose: to misuse power. Abusing your power is to use your power to control other people. But a good use of power is to use your power to empower other people. Using our power negatively will result in controlling other people. This is a major factor at work in creating inequity between male and female relationships.

The Duluth Model is an inventory used by a national hotline that asks some key questions about how we use our power.[6] Use these questions as a personal reflection tool as you think about the way you use your own power.

Coercion and Threats (misuse of power) versus Negotiation and Fairness (good use of power):

- Are you kind to those you lead?
- Are you treating them well?
- Are you fair in the decisions that impact them?
- Do you seek mutually satisfying solutions to conflict?

- Can you accept change?
- Are you willing to compromise?

Intimidation (misuse of power) versus Nonthreatening Behavior (good use of power):

- Do you cut people off when they are talking?
- Do you dismiss ideas?
- Do you close yourself off from interaction or feedback?
- Do you talk and act so that people feel comfortable expressing themselves and doing things?

Emotional Abuse (misuse of power) versus Respect (good use of power):

- Do you value and actively listen to others?
- Do you show regard for other people's traditions/opinions/feelings/experiences?
- Are you emotionally affirming?

Isolation (misuse of power) versus Trust and Support (good use of power):

- Do you encourage people to think and act widely?
- Is there room to grow and participate in self-improvement?
- Do people feel included in decision-making processes?

Minimizing, Denying, and Blaming (misuse of power) versus Honesty and Accountability (good use of power):

- Do you accept responsibility for yourself?
- Do you acknowledge when you've been wrong?
- Do you communicate openly and honestly?
- Do you have people in your life who can challenge your behavior?

Economic Abuse (misuse of power) versus Economic Partnership (good use of power):

- Have you mutually agreed with others about fair distribution of work?
- Do you make decisions with others?
- Is everyone economically compensated fairly and equally?

Male Privilege (misuse of power) versus Shared Responsibility (good use of power):

- Are women invited to be part of big decisions?
- Do you treat women as subservient (like a servant)?
- Do you define the role women and/or men play in your culture?

Power is such an important part of equity that I think we need to dig a little deeper. Discovering the power you do have and asking how you use it are essential in changing your practices around power. But I think we can go deeper still. I believe that the way we view power is often unhelpful.

Does Power Corrupt?

Most of us have more or less agreed with the idea that power corrupts. This quote by Lord Acton writing to Bishop Creighton in 1887 has summed up the way this generation views power: "Power tends to corrupt and absolute power corrupts absolutely. Great men are almost always bad men."[7] I think Lord Acton had a cynical view of power, or maybe it was an accurate view from his experience. But the question about corruption and power is an important one. Is power always a corrupting agent? I don't think so. But I think I know how we get to that understanding. We have corrupted views on what power is and what power is for. Consider these three ideas around power.

Power is corrupting if you view it as a limited resource. In other words, if you think that there is a finite amount of power to hold, then getting that power will be a corrupting influence. But what if power isn't a limited resource? How would that change the way we view it?

Power is corrupting if you view it as a means to control other people or events. What if power was less about control and more about influence? This question is perhaps the most important one at the heart of the social revolution ignited by the internet. What if true power is influence and not control?

Power is corrupting if you think it's yours. What if power is infinite and influential *and a gift*? What if power doesn't belong to us? What if power is a gift that we are called to use and not possess? What if true power is about stewardship and not ownership?

Jesus is the most powerful human to have ever lived. If you hold to the Christian teachings of his origins, you will know that he came from "above." He was with God and is God (John 1:1–3). Jesus left the comforts and riches and power of heaven to descend in earthly form (as a human) with a redemption plan. He wanted to reveal God to the world. What is God like? Who is God? How does God feel/act/relate? All the deep questions humanity had about their Creator, Jesus came to answer. He came in human form to demonstrate what God is like, who God is, and how God lives. Jesus helped humanity discover their original purpose and callings. What does it mean to be human? How should humans feel/act/relate?

Jesus had absolute power—more power than anyone in the created cosmos (beyond what we even know exists). *But Jesus was not corrupted by power.* As a matter of fact, if you read the account of Jesus from every angle, you will discover something remarkable about his relationship to power. Jesus *gave power away.* You could sum up Jesus' ministry with that statement. Jesus came to give power away. And I think the reason Jesus could have so much power and not be corrupted by it is because he understood better than anyone that power is not a finite resource; it's infinite. Because power at its best is not about control—it's about influence. Jesus wielded power to great effect.

Napoleon Bonaparte was amazed by the kind of influence Jesus had. Hundreds of years later he said, "I know men; and I tell you that Jesus Christ is no mere man. Between Him and every person in the world there is no possible term of comparison. Alexander, Caesar, Charlemagne, and I have founded empires. But on what did we rest the creations of our genius? Upon force. Jesus Christ founded His empire upon love; and at this hour millions of men would die for him."[8]

The person of Jesus helps us shift our perspective on power. It challenges our previously held fear-based mind-set that believes if you give your power away, you will have less of it. But is that true? Did Jesus lose power as he gave it away?

Think about it. Even at the start of the creation account, God gave humans choice. The capacity and freedom to choose is knit into the fabric of our humanity. If power were about control and God is all-powerful, he would not have given humans choice. To give humans choice (even while knowing that they were going to use their choice to distance themselves from him) was an incredibly questionable decision if power is control. But if power is influence, it's an incredibly important one. See, true power is the ability to influence people to identify the power they have and to use it for others.

There is a fantastic story at the end of Jesus' ministry when he took the towel of a servant and began to wash the disciples' feet. He taught them, as he washed their feet, that he was calling them to a type of leadership that was remarkably different from what they had known. It's "servant leadership." The foot-washing passage is often used as an example of humility and service. This is true, but there are some parts of the story that also help us in our discussion about power.

The context of the story is key. It starts with this declaration: "Because Jesus knew that all authority had been given to him, where he had come from and where he was going, he took off his outer garment and took a servant's towel" (John 13:3–4, my paraphrase). Did you catch that? Jesus had identified his power. He was not ashamed or in denial or pretending. Far from posturing himself as having no power, he was in full awareness of his power. He knew where he was from and where he was headed. Jesus was not afraid. When he stood before Pilate a few days later, condemned and beaten, Pilate tried to convince Jesus to defend himself. Jesus would not speak. Pilate tried to compel him, saying, "You should talk to me because I have the power to kill you." You can almost hear Jesus laugh. Jesus responded to Pilate to remind him that the only power he held was the power God gave. In other words, Jesus spelled out for Pilate the way true power works—you don't *have* power, you *use* it.

Back to Jesus washing the disciples' feet. Peter put up a fuss. He instinctively felt uncomfortable because what Jesus was doing was outside of the normal structure for the rabbi/student power dynamic. Peter blurted out that he didn't want Jesus to wash his feet. And then another thing happened. Jesus said to Peter, "Unless you let me wash your feet, you will have no part of me" (John 13:9, my paraphrase). Which, let's be honest, seems a little harsh. What was happening? Why the crazy reaction?

Jesus was trying to communicate the dynamic of *using your power to influence without fear.* And in order for power to be used without fear, it has to be anchored in and saturated with love. The way that power is used as a tool for influence toward positive change is through love. Instinctively, we tend to share Peter's resistance. We think that power is strong and love is soft. So Peter was basically not interested in soft, feeling-based relationship—he was interested in power. But Jesus messed up his categories. He changed the way the game was played; it's a revolution of power. The most powerful leader ever was serving the disciples not to prove a point but to use his power to influence his disciples toward living lives of love.

Power and Love

The reason Jesus is the perfect picture of power is that he is both power and love personified. Love, far from just an emotional feeling, is an eternal force for transformation.

Theologian Paul Tillich defined power as "the drive of everything living to realize itself" and love as "the drive towards the unity of the separated."[9]

Power and love were the subjects of one of the most poignant sermons by the brilliant mind of Martin Luther King Jr., who understood these two forces as being deeply and divinely connected to create redemptive change in the world. He put it like this: "Power without love is reckless and abusive, and love without power is sentimental and anemic."

King also said, "When I speak of love I am not speaking of some sentimental and weak response. I am speaking of that force which all of the great religions have seen as the supreme unifying principle of life. Love is somehow the key that unlocks the door which leads to ultimate reality."[10]

This explains why Jesus was able to bring such transformation to the world after only a few short years of ministry. Jesus perfectly balanced his power with love. Nowhere is this more imperative than in relationships. To love others is to empower them. And to empower others is to love them. That is what makes the topic of gender equity so profound and so difficult. You can make legislative changes that will benefit women (and I think we should continue to do so), but that is only what equality demands. What mutual flourishing requires is power matched with love.

When Adam Kahane researched the use of power and love for effective change in global social issues, he concluded that they are not opposites, although they hold space at seemingly polarized places. Rather than choosing one, Kahane suggested that we must opt for both. "Love and power are not options that we can choose between; they are complementary poles and we must choose both." He said the best image for understanding the nature between power and love is breathing. If you only exercise power, you are exhaling. You can exhale for a while but not forever because, well, you will die. Power will corrupt and destroy. But the inhale is love. Again, you can inhale deeply, but if that's all you do, you die. A regular pattern of inhaling and exhaling will result in a healthy body. You will live. And the better you get at breathing, the better your life becomes. Likewise, a regular habit of using power (force for self-realization) with love (unifying the separated) will bring life to all of us.[11]

Power is influence and influence is power. If everyone used their power to benefit others, what would happen? Think about this in terms of relationships. If you love your wife, do you love your children less? If you love your children, do you love your mother less? No. Love expands.

Power is also an infinite, unlimited resource. So is influence. If you influence someone, your influence doesn't diminish—it expands. Just like love. Power and love are meant to be wings helping the bird of change to fly. Empowerment (love and power) is the way to change the world. Great leaders use power to empower other people.

The Empowerment Principle

No matter what you believe about who Jesus was (and is), I think we might all agree that his life changed the world forever. How did he do it? As the greatest leader who ever lived, he changed the world by empowering people. He saw everyone and every opportunity through the lens of imagination and faith. He literally went around giving away power. Nowhere is this more revolutionary in the life of Jesus than in his interactions with women. Jesus invited women to discipleship at a time when women couldn't even sit in the same room as men. He asked them for help in a blatant disregard of the general bias against women; he treated them as leaders and partners in telling everyone about this new kingdom that was dismantling systems of injustice, prejudice, sexism, racism, and classism—and every other kind of ism! That is possible not just because of who Jesus was but because of how Jesus lived. Jesus showed us how to live our lives by using his power to empower other people.

This is important to understand because true poverty is not just about economics; it's about power. The definition of poverty is disempowerment. This means that how you use the power you do have is the measure of your leadership. Think about how this could work for women in the workplace. Sheryl Sandberg's organization Lean In suggests that men stepping up to use their power to mentor women "will ultimately lead to stronger and safer workplaces for everyone. When more women are in leadership, organizations offer employees more generous policies and produce better business results."[12] Not only that, but when organizations hire more women, sexual harassment rates are considerably lower. It's time to start recognizing our power and using it for others.

Things to Think About

- Have you identified the power you do have?
- How do you use your power to benefit others?
- Would you say you have a healthy balance of love and power?
- What areas are difficult for you to use your power well?
- Who is an example of an empowering leader in your life?

PART THREE

How We Get There

ELEVEN

Stopping the Blame Game

A pure heart is necessary to see God in each other.
If you see God in each other, there is love for each
other, then there is peace.

—MOTHER TERESA

I spent many years living in a community of drug addicts. In this area over seven thousand addicts were living in eight city blocks. Because the drug problem (heroin) had become so intensely pervasive, the city had declared a health emergency. Over 90 percent of the residents of the neighborhood were HIV positive and over 70 percent had hepatitis C. To prevent the spread of infectious diseases, the government made it possible for the addicts of the neighborhood to use freely (and even with supervision) without any fear of getting arrested. The only condition was that they weren't allowed to use outside the eight-block radius allocated by the city. This situation made the already difficult realities of addiction, accompanied by the plethora of other challenges like homelessness, mental illness, sexual exploitation, and violence, unbearable. To this day the community remains a living hell for many of its residents.

It's difficult to find solutions to the ongoing problems because every conversation is rooted in trying to find and assign blame for the situation. I understand this temptation very well because I was furious with the "harm reduction" strategists who insisted that clean needles and nurse supervision at free injection sites would offer dignity to addicts, especially while watching their lives continue to spiral into death. I was convinced the city had made a massively unjust decision about a population that was economically expendable. I was infuriated at the constant stream of men who drove from every suburb in that beautiful city to further exploit and dehumanize female addicts desperate for a fix. I spent many years pointing my finger and trying to find out whose fault it was that this neighborhood was so broken.

The truth of the matter is that all that blaming led nowhere. Did people share responsibility for decisions and injustices? Yes, of course. We all did. If the truth be told, every person in that city bore some responsibility for the conditions of the community. But so what? Where does that get us? I could actually spend my entire lifetime looking for a culprit for the kind of oppression I witnessed in that area—but in the end I'd be in the exact same place that I started.

The Blame Game

A strong human tendency when a problem becomes unearthed is to assign blame. I think on some level assigning blame gives us a sense of control and closure. Like we've done something. Consider the cultural delight in scapegoating: we find examples of the situation, point them out, and then declare that they've been dealt with because we've treated the scapegoat with extreme punishment. Like once "that person" or "that situation" is dealt with, the matter is done, allowing us to believe that what has happened is an outside problem, not an inside one.

Audre Lorde spoke to this tendency to see oppression as something happening outside of us when she pinpointed what's really necessary. "The true focus of revolutionary change is never merely the oppressive situations which we seek to escape, but that piece of the oppressor which is planted deep within each of us."[1]

There are many reasons we get sucked into the blame game. Dr. Susan Krauss Whitbourne suggested five. I think they bear repeating:

Blame is an excellent defense mechanism. Whether you call it projection, denial, or displacement, blame helps you preserve your sense of self-esteem by avoiding awareness of your own flaws or failings.

Blame is a tool we use when we're in attack mode. Falling into the category of a destructive conflict resolution method, blame is a way to try to hurt our partners.

We're not very good at figuring out the causes of other people's behavior, or even our own. The attributions we make, whether to luck or ability, can be distorted by our tendency to make illogical judgments. And we're just as bad at making judgments involving the blameworthiness of actions in terms of intent vs. outcome.

It's easier to blame someone else than to accept responsibility. There's less effort involved in recognizing your contributions to a bad situation than in accepting the fact that you're actually at fault, and changing so you don't do it again.

People lie. . . . "Everybody lies." It's pretty easy just to lie and blame someone else even though you know you're at fault. You may figure that no one will know it was really you who spilled coffee all over the break room, so you just blame someone else who's not there (and hope that person never finds out).[2]

There is a revolutionary story in the life of Jesus (John 9:1–8) where he was walking with his disciples and they saw a man born blind. The disciples asked Jesus, "Whose fault is it that this man was born blind? Was it his sin or his parents'?" (my paraphrase). The disciples had no other worldview except that suffering was a result of sin. *Someone was to blame.*

They are not alone. I think especially in the conversation around women and men, we are always looking for blame. Whose fault is it that women have been treated unfairly for generations? Culture? Society? Men? The devil? Eve? Just a quick read of Mary Beard's book *Women & Power* is infuriating. She unearths the roots of misogyny and sexism in the history of Western civilization starting at the very epicenter of cultural progress.

I think the fault we are looking for is not so much the individual responsibility (although healing the wounds will require some admission and restitution and changed behavior, but more on that later). If we have our minds set on looking for blame, I think the fault we will actually find is a crack in the foundations of our world. It's a brokenness at the heart of creation that goes all the way back to our first parents. It traces back to the beginning. If we are looking for blame, we will always be looking backward. That should tell us something.

When the disciples walking alongside Jesus asking the question about whose fault it was, Jesus responded, "It isn't this man's sin or his parents'. This man was born blind for the glory of God!" (v. 3, my paraphrase). No one expected that. No one could even comprehend what he meant. In those days sin and suffering were equated. It was always someone's fault.

Have a quick read through the book of Job or Ecclesiastes and you will recongize how existential the world becomes if there is no one to blame. I mean, in some respects the whole #MeToo and #TimesUp movements are about exposing the people who have done the deed. It's outing the ones responsible. And to be sure, without accountability for actions, darkness will fester and grow. An unchecked leader is a dangerous one.

But the disciples weren't looking to change things; they were trying to find an excuse to live with them. And that's what Jesus was trying to shift. What's the point of finding blame if you aren't prepared to change? Jesus didn't look backward; he was always looking forward. He was always saying and doing things that ushered in the future. Jesus reframed the whole situation.

What if we look ahead instead of behind? What if we move from a *why* to a *what now*? It is crucial to ask the right question right now. No longer "Whose fault is it?" but "What can we do?"

What if this current situation is not about finding fault or blame in the past but is an opportunity to change the future? Now that's worth talking about. Once Jesus changed the focus, you can feel the situation shift from a theoretical one to an expectant one. Now, everyone was paying attention because what was a "too hard and too late" conversation became a place of possibility.

"Whose fault is it?" is a paralyzing, fear-based, and frankly useless question when it comes to changing the way women and men work together. But how could our healing, wholeness, and restoration be woven into a story that brings glory to God? That's a question worth asking and living. What if we focused on the future instead of the past? Learning from our past is a great idea, but getting stuck in the perpetual rehashing of it to find blame is always counterproductive. Let's think about what we can do about the future.

If we will take a clue from Jesus, we will reframe suffering and tragedy into possibility and hope. Instead of liability, we can choose to see an opportunity to bring light and healing into this present moment.

Changing the Narrative

In 2011 I wrote *The Liberating Truth*, a book about how Jesus empowered women.[3] It is a glimpse at the beautiful way Jesus lived his life and the amazing, truly revolutionary way he treated, interacted with, and invited women into the redemption story. His behavior gave hints about what restoration will look like when we lose the fear, stop hunting for the blame, and start living into the opportunity to heal everyone and everything—including our relationships.

But it's not enough to admire Jesus. It's not even enough to point out how he lived and corrected so many imbalances and confronted so many injustices just by living differently. It's not enough to even agree with him. We must *participate*. In the story we explored from John 9, Jesus said to his disciples, "We must quickly carry out the work assigned to us!" (my paraphrase). I'm certain he was not using the royal "we." He was not on a solo mission, content with forever being the exception to the rules of social restraint and prejudice and racism and sexism and exclusivity. He was inviting his disciples to quickly be about the work of seeing terrible, unjust, dark, and dreary things as opportunities for God to shine. It's not enough to just see the possibilities; we must seize them.

That's why a defensive posture is so unhelpful. If we are stuck hiding or defending or in the corner of our "gender," we can't get to the *what now?* And we need to get there urgently.

I believe gender inequity is at the heart of the world's greatest felt needs. And there is an answer. Reconciliation is pulsing as a kingdom idea that will meet the deepest needs of our time. But do we dare take the moment in front of us and demonstrate what healing looks like?

Think about it. Just one man at the side of the road allowed Jesus to shift perspective, change his posture, and extend healing that began to unravel the tapestry for everyone. For the disciples, their biases were exposed, their religious sensibilities were renewed, their understanding of God's power was realigned. For the blind man, healing equaled choices, contribution, inclusion, and genuine dignity.

And to us, who are rethinking our own systemic prejudice and judgment, thousands of years later, we, too, are challenged to reevaluate and relearn how Jesus influences our relationships, our ideas, our cultural norms. One man. Posture shift. Open eyes for everyone! He is the light of the world. And I've got a hunch when Jesus tells us that we are the light of the world, it will look a bit like that. Opening eyes for everyone. Do you see sin? I see glory! Do you see blame? I see opportunity! Do you see the past (failure, pain)? I see the future (hope, healing)! Light of the world streaming into the darkness of a finding-fault era.

Rather than pit women against men or men against women, perhaps it's time to shift our allegiances altogether. To avoid the binary us-versus-them framework that has kept us divided. Let's join forces and fight the real enemy: the blindness of culture, inequity, gender bias, abuse, harassment, and fear. We will need one another to participate in a whole new framework of unity that culminates in open eyes and fresh living.

The Original Design

The most incredible origin story of humanity is found in the Hebrew Torah, as well as the first book of the Bible, Genesis. Scholars believe it was written at a time when the Israelites had been in and out of captivity and slavery so many times that they had started to believe that oppression was normal. Almost every other creation story from other cultures at that time told about one leader (the supreme ruler) who was made "in the image of God" and then the rest of humanity was made to serve the gods through that ruler. The writer of Genesis told a revolutionary story. He told a story that suggests that *all of humanity* (women and men) were created "in the image of God" (1:27) and were created to be together.

Now, to suggest that this was a revolutionary idea is to miss the sheer audacity of the author of Genesis. Men and women both made in the image of God—together! In this remarkable story, men and women, in a shared leadership model, are given the task to co-steward the earth. It's a picture of perfection. There is no shame, fear, disunity, or violence. Everything is working in perfect harmony, including men and women together, sharing leadership. We were made this way, said the author of Genesis, for equality, freedom, mutuality, and leadership. The reason we have the longing to live a better story is because we were designed for it.

If you read the whole account of creation in the Genesis story, you will also find that there was a time when God acknowledged that something wasn't good in his creation. It's a pretty straightforward rhythm: "God said" and then he saw and declared, "This is good." But one time and only one time he saw that it wasn't good. Now, to be sure, it doesn't mean that what he created wasn't good—the word for *good* used in the Genesis account is more comparable to "complete." In other words, God saw that what he had created wasn't finished. It needed something more. The moment in creation where God said "It isn't good" was when he created man and man was alone. The only time in the creation of the cosmos where God said, "Oh no, this won't work" was when man was leading everything by himself. This is important. God was not saying that men aren't good. He was saying that men are not designed to be alone. One is the loneliest number.

This is fascinating to me. We never hear about this. As a matter of fact, we have created management systems and boards and businesses and churches and nonprofits with a man at the top, leading, alone. Now, to be sure, there are teams around him and whole companies to help, but ultimately the top dog, the senior leader, the grand pooh-bah, is almost always a man. By himself. The very thing God said was *not good* about his creation project is what we continue to do. Is it any wonder that men who lead alone face such harsh realities, including severe loneliness, depression, addiction, broken relationships, and isolation? I feel like it's worth going back to the original blueprint. Maybe there is something in the foundation that needs to be fixed. Might it be worth revisiting the entrenched idea that it always has to be lonely at the top? Maybe instead of loneliness being the inevitable cost of great leadership, we could rethink our options. Maybe there is another way of doing leadership. A better way?

It's never a bad idea to take a page out of God's best designs. And what God did when Adam was alone was create a helpmate, which in the original Hebrew is the term *ezer*. *Ezer* means a tutor, a helper, a savior, a deliverer. Most of the other times the word is used in Scripture, it refers to the actions of God saving Israel from difficult or impossible situations. God discovered that there was a better way to lead and so created the best leadership model—men and women together.

This is mind-blowing. Not only is this original design the answer for women who feel limited and stuck and outside of the leadership zone. It's also the answer for men who feel lonely, overworked, exhausted, and stuck on the wheel of production and provision. God's original best-case design is for a shared leadership structure. A team model. Shared responsibility.

How would team leadership as a best model shift our understanding of leading? I've never been more convinced that this is a problem that has a divine answer. And it's an answer that will liberate us all. When God finished making Eve as an *ezer* for Adam, the declaration was no longer just good; it was very good (v. 31). It's a high point of the created order. This would be a fantastic time for us to pay attention. Are we still aiming for the "best we can do" scenario based on a sin-infused world? I think we should aim for the best creation strategy God gave us—a shared humanity. A shared leadership.

The Best Strategy

The way we were designed for each other is deeply connected to who God is. And the way we think about God is at the root of our relationships. In chapter 8 we talked about how our mind-set affects the way we see and do everything else. This is especially true about God. This is not a theology book, but how we view God is relevant because what we believe shapes what we value, and what we value shapes what we do, and inevitably what we do dictates what happens in our lives. So what we believe about one another and the world and the future and God matters in every single decision we make. Let's break it down to get clarity on how this relates to gender.

God is not male. God is not female. *God transcends gender.* Much like God transcends time. It's not that God doesn't work through gender; we can see this in the creation of humanity and then in every woman and man used to advance the kingdom of God throughout history. There are many of them, both male and female.

It's important to reemphasize this point. This is not a fight about whether God is male or female. But the fact that we only refer to all the aspects of the Trinity as male is evidence of a prejudice at work in the undercurrent of our belief system. And that matters.

I was at a leadership conference recently and referred to the Holy Spirit in the feminine. I said a lot of other things as well, things I thought would be helpful and relevant to leaders—things about violence and justice and hope for the next generation. But the emails I received about that talk were from men who felt uncomfortable with me referring to the Holy Spirit as "she." Which is interesting. Women never write to me upset that I refer to God as "he." Women only ever hear God described as male, and when they suggest it feels exclusive and/or hard to digest, they are labeled as liberal and offensive. But when some men hear God referred to in the feminine, they lash out at the sense of exclusion. They feel insulted. They can't relate.

Now, I'm not trying to make everyone refer to God as "she" or insist on gender-inclusive language. I'm just pointing out that the fact that we have a problem with this idea reveals a deep theological bias in the way we think about God. This is more important than we may at first realize. In our temptation to swat away an irritating little fly of gender inclusivity, we dismiss these ideas and attitudes as though they don't really matter. The problem is they are the way we identify that something much deeper is rotting within our belief system. We think God is male. I know we say we don't. But we do. How could we not?

The important point to understand is that God is not limited by one gender but is understood and revealed through *both together*. The emphasis was never meant to be put on one gender but on relationship. The bride of Christ is the church because God wanted to emphasize that what he was after more than anything else was relationship, love, covenant, connection, and intimacy. Something we could refer to as "mutual thriving." This is deeply connected to the original creation account when God saw that it wasn't good for man to be alone—emphasis on *alone*. When God created humanity, God said, "Let *us* make mankind in *our* image" (v. 26, emphasis added). In other words, God wasn't alone either. God is not lonely. God is not male. God is not female. God is community. God is relationship. God is love. God is Trinity. This is a mystery that we've largely ignored because we are busy making

God a CEO who manages his time effectively and delegates to subordinates. God does not lead alone; he leads in community. *This should not only challenge us with regard to how we view God, but it should also radically redefine our leadership styles.*

A friend and mentor told me about the controversy surrounding the decision they made in 2001 to update the NIV translation. At the helm was a man, a father who was reading the Scriptures with his family over the dining room table when his daughter expressed her feelings of exclusion. They were discussing an epistle that began by saying "Brothers," which is how Paul was addressing the church. The father explained to his daughter that the original Greek word was inclusive and that without a doubt Paul was addressing all believers at the church, which definitely included her. She asked him, "If that is the case, then why doesn't the English Bible just say that?"

It suddenly dawned on him how important it was to pay attention to inclusion in a Bible translation. Which is why during the most recent NIV update, he asked the translation team to be as faithful to the original text as possible in those areas where the English translation lacked language inclusivity. The goal was a better reflection of the original intention of the text.[4] They did not attempt to identify any person of God as female. It was already going to be a big deal to translate the original text to its actual original meaning. They were right. There was an immediate uproar from American Christians who suggested that by using inclusive language the NIV had ruined the Bible and that they were on a liberal agenda to destroy the church.

This itself is curious. And it exposes a bias at the heart of what we think about God that is important to pay attention to. But even more crucial to this conversation about destiny and design is an essential revelation of God. God is Trinity. God is not alone. God does not work in a top-down hierarchical vortex of absolute power. God is community. God is relationship. God is shared leadership. God is relational. God is all the things that gender equity will help us create on earth.

We will reflect our understanding of God in the way we lead. We were designed to do this. The way we lead will demonstrate to others what God is like. And what is God like? Do you see how these things are connected?

God transcends gender, using all the incredible feminine qualities and all the amazing masculine aspects in a combination of mutual flourishing that overflows with love. That is what makes the return to a peace-filled world possible. Everything in the created order is longing for that original purpose to be restored. Everything. And the way that order is restored is through right relationships. Leadership needs to be done not just *for* God but *like* God. The essence of godly leadership is shared, mutual, and flourishing.

So back to the side of a dirt road outside a village in ancient Israel with Jesus and the disciples. Jesus shifted the focus from blame to glory. And this is an important detail. He said, "This man was born blind for the glory of God" (my paraphrase). And it was no mistake. In so many ways Jesus was peeling back the oppression that has veiled our sight from the intention God has always had for us. Glory is about essence. Glory is the "stuff" God is made of. Glory is a loaded word about power and value.

Jesus was talking about getting back something that's been lost through sin and brokenness. Jesus was restoring the original plan of God to reveal his glory through humanity. Through us.

We don't have to spend one more minute on blame. We can follow Jesus' example and look for the glory that exists in the original design of who we were always meant to be. Together, we are the glory of God revealed in this world. Let's live that way.

Things to Think About

- Do you recognize this time as an opportunity or a threat? Why?
- Are you taking sides or assigning blame? How could you change your perspective/posture?
- Are you sensing the urgency?
- How can you participate in uncovering the glory of God in people around you?

TWELVE

Start Now and with You

I'd do anything for the perfect body—except diet
and exercise.

—JAY LENO

t's easy to point the finger at other places and other people. But
the reality is that change begins with us, right now. "Tomorrow
never happens," sang Janis Joplin. "It's all the same day."[1]
And she's more right than we might have first thought. Jesus
reminded us of the power of the present when he said, "The time
has come" (Mark 1:15). Starting is an urgent and present message. The work of beginning is always a current one. And let's
be honest—putting it off until a more opportune time usually
means not doing it at all. If we really want to change, we must
begin. As Martin Luther King Jr. said, "Justice too long delayed
is justice denied."

Companies report that they are highly committed to gender diversity. But that commitment has not translated into meaningful progress. The proportion of women at every level in corporate America has hardly changed. Progress isn't just slow. It's stalled.

That's what they found in *Women in the Workplace 2018*, "a study conducted by McKinsey in partnership with LeanIn.org. In the fourth year of . . . ongoing research, [they probed] the issues, drawing on data from 279 companies employing more than 13 million people, as well as on a survey of over 64,000 employees and a series of qualitative interviews."[2]

The study found that "women are doing their part. For more than 30 years, they've been earning more bachelor's degrees than men. They're asking for promotions and negotiating salaries at the same rates as men. And contrary to conventional wisdom, they are staying in the workforce at the same rate as men."[3] So what's the problem? The problem is that even though people understand gender equity to be a great idea, they just aren't doing it.

Companies need to take more decisive action. This starts with treating gender diversity like the business priority it is, from setting targets to holding leaders accountable for results. It requires closing gender gaps in hiring and promotions, especially early in the pipeline when women are most often overlooked. And it means taking bolder steps to create a respectful and inclusive culture so women—and all employees—feel safe and supported at work.[4]

Jeff Lockyear, the pastor who transitioned his male-dominated leadership team to a shared model, talked about it this way: "If you're a church leader, just because you don't intend to exclude doesn't mean you intentionally include."[5]

Discovering Solutions

Many years ago I was invited to a banking conference in downtown Vancouver with the HSBC. It was a bit of a detour from my usual life of ministry, advocating for the poor and speaking to Christian groups. I had been chosen as a woman of influence in the community and was asked to address the audience of hundreds of female banking professionals on the keys to effective leadership. I was amazed at the idea of a banking conference for women bankers. Over lunch I asked the western manager of HSBC how and why this event was happening. He explained that, several years before, the company realized they had been losing their best managers. After spending considerable time, effort, and energy recruiting and retraining new managers to replace them, the executives asked themselves a different question: "Where did they go?" They began an inquiry with the former managers to discover why they had left and also to determine if they might return. That process revealed some fascinating information for the bank about gender and inclusion. The first thing they discovered (when they took the time to look) was that the vast majority of the managers they were losing were female. A range of issues was discovered that prevented women from advancing and staying with the bank the way it was.

Fast-forward to their employment report in 2017: "We strive to make HSBC a great place to work and we're proud of our inclusive, positive and customer-first work culture." Some highlights of their accomplishments are a board of directors that has equally represented men and women since 2013, their first female president and CEO (2015), and 60 percent of all senior leadership positions are held by women.[6]

Wow. They changed their mind-set, smashed the glass ceiling, created new practices and policies, and are reaping the results. The Canadian HSBC is better than ever. The CEO and president put it like this: "I firmly believe our strong business performance is directly attributable to our commitment to creating and sustaining an inclusive workforce and workplace. HSBC's agility in responding to client and market needs exceeds my expectations and reflects the diversity of our engaged and empowered workforce."[7]

So how did they do it?

They've been on the journey for a while. But how they began matters. We tend to overcomplicate things when it comes to implementation. So I'm going to offer a simple tool to help us move forward. Amplify Peace developed this tool to help move people toward internal and community change. Although very simple, it's not easy. But the results of moving deeper into the process will allow ongoing transformation to occur.

1. Listen. We are intentionally listening to voices that are not easily heard *and* we are listening to understand them better. This will require our paying attention to who is excluded from our community and influence, seeking out the voices that are marginalized in our community, and then becoming intentional about seeking them out. This will also mean we will work on our ability to truly understand other people's stories.

The first thing that HSBC did and that anyone can do to move toward mutual thriving is to listen. The most transformational way to listen is to pay attention to the voices that are not at the table. If women are not in your leadership team, then start asking questions to the right people. Find the women who should be leading and ask them about it. And here is the hardest part about this step: *really listen*. Our tendency is to try to fix the problem immediately or to get defensive. Practice makes perfect in this regard.

Adam Kahane is a director of Reos Partners, an international social enterprise that helps people move forward together on their most important and intractable issues. Many times he has faced the challenge of getting things done that really matter while trying to get people who don't trust one another to work together. In his experience listening is the most important strategy. He suggested four basic forms of listening:

- **Downloading:** Getting more information. Hearing people talk. Reading books.
- **Debating:** Considering all the angles. Hearing from all sides of the situation.
- **Critical thinking:** Challenging thought.
- **Dialoguing:** Talking it through. Asking questions. Discovering more.[8]

Although all the forms of listening are valid and important when it comes to transformation, this one is the key: *presencing*. This form of listening transforms. This kind of listening invites us to stop critiquing and debating (even internally) and start to "be with" the person who is sharing. There is a Native American proverb that says you can't understand another person's journey until you have walked a mile in their moccasins. Presencing is allowing yourself to enter into the other person's experience. To be part of the pain and the joy. This is the most transformational stage of listening and the hardest one to allow yourself to do.

2. Learn. Curiosity is much more powerful than judgment. A learning posture is an open one. For peace to come we must seek to find new ways of navigating this world. Instead of joining one side or another, we listen. We lean in. We seek new ways to engage in the narratives of others.

Be curious. In a conversation, how often are you the one asking the questions, truly wanting to hear and learn from the other person? When curiosity begins to define our lives, we become lifelong learners of how things work and how they can change. We become open to the theoretical possibilities of change. Hopeful even that things can change.

Are you okay with not always having an answer? Sometimes there are no solutions or answers and we must learn to sit in those spaces of unknown, uncertainty, and in the land in between. Learning to embrace these situations can be disrupting and uncomfortable but also freeing.

There are ways of changing structures and systems to adapt toward a thriving, equitable workplace. After listening to their top female managers who had left the bank, HSBC realized that inflexibility in the structure of their employment model was a barrier. They discovered there was a lot more room to experiment with workplace flexibility than they had ever thought. The digital realities of today, other employee models of flexible or staggered work hours, outcome drivers over time clocks—as they discovered these new ways of working, not only did they gain back female employees, but all employees benefited.

One of the key areas of learning will be in our management of work and family balance. HSBC (and many other companies) have noted the realities of work/family stress on employees. According to the research, women still bear the burden of domestic work while also trying to advance in their careers. Old paradigms demanding sixty to eighty hours a week of work time are unsustainable and unrealistic for parents. So what to do?

Creating new systems rewarding a job well done and also allowing for the proper placement of family is not only a good idea; it's one that will help all employees to thrive. Studies show that both women and men thrive when their work and family life can go together. Things like parental leave and flexible schedules have vastly improved the health, well-being, and outcomes of employees. A thriving workplace will want to ensure the health of its employees as well as maximize the outcome and sustainability of its best people.

To learn from the best, let's start right now with the five tactical measures that have the biggest impact on increasing gender diversity in corporations' top management:

- Visible monitoring of gender-diversity programs by CEO, executive team
- Flexible working conditions, locations
- Programs to reconcile work and family life
- Senior executives mentoring junior women
- Programs encouraging female networking and role models[9]

3. Live. Taking the theory of change and transferring it into our everyday lives takes deliberate attention. Once we have listened and learned new ways of seeing and engaging in mutually flourishing relationships, it is up to us to make the necessary adjustments to our own areas of influence. Living differently based on what we have discovered will be essential to change.

It's not enough to want things to change. We have to commit to implement real changes in our practices to ensure it. Studies suggest that getting the basics right (creating targets for inclusion with regular reporting and accountability to meet them), ensuring hiring and promotions are fair, equipping senior leaders to be champions of diversity, fostering a respectful culture, making the "only" experience rare, and offering employees flexibility are all proven and effective strategies you could implement right now.[10]

Do you have measures for gender equity in your community? Are you even aiming for it?

Getting It Done

Without an implementation of actual goals, you will not see change. "As church leaders, we need to be honest about whether a vision of holistic leadership is being realized," said Pastor Jeff Lockyear. "We need to be sober about the blind spots of why what should happen isn't happening. And we need to commit to *deliberately doing different things and doing things differently* in order to get different results instead of propagating the definition of insanity and continuing to do the same while expecting different."[11]

One of the key components of Jeff Lockyear's success was using concrete measurement tools for gender equity as they started the process of change and for several years after. He explained,

Around the same time that we launched these initiatives, we started participating in a staff-wide employee engagement survey. That first year there was a stark difference in the experience of our men and women, with women scoring barely above the survey's statistical benchmark of toxic. Our 2018 survey, for the first time, scored women's experience of our workplace higher than men—far beyond the statistical threshold for flourishing. And it's not just the women who are benefiting. In total, that 2013 survey registered the church at the bare minimum of what they qualify as a healthy workplace, where now for the past two years we've registered in the top 1 percent of organizations to have ever taken the survey. As we actively pursue this vision of empowerment—described in our language as "spiritual Moms and spiritual Dads parenting the family together"—our whole family is winning![12]

When Jeff's church started this project, they had a coach. Ellen Duffield helped the church work on two strategies to implement changes. First, they made a "disproportionate investment" into women's confidence and leadership. Because they took the time to listen and to learn, they realized that without a strategic investment into the empowerment of women there would be no shift in their culture. Using small groups of training and resources, they developed the talent they already had. At the same time they started a strategic initiative for leadership development for girls right at that confidence-eroding age (eleven to thirteen)—shaping the next generation of girls to become leaders who thrive. The results have been extraordinary.

The second implementation Jeff's team employed was to provide "disproportionate invitation." Seeking to change the "court" of the culture of their work environment so women don't have to live in an exclusively man's world, they implemented some strategic steps.

They started to actively reach out and invite women into leadership challenges, especially in areas where they saw competence and hesitancy.

They committed to invite women into conversations—to express their voice where they wouldn't naturally assert themselves or compete for attention.

They set a 30 percent mandatory minimum female presence for women to feel comfortable expressing their voice (this is based on research showing women will not always thrive as an "exception" but will flourish with at least 30 percent representation).

The research suggests that when too few women are present at the leadership table, it results in an "only" syndrome. They have a significantly worse experience than women who work with more women. They often feel on guard, pressured to perform, and left out. They are also almost twice as likely to have been sexually harassed during the course of their career.[13]

Experts in gender diversity promote the 30 percent minimum guideline as a way to avoid tokenism and affect cultural change. Gender and the Economy reported, "Research suggests that insisting on a critical mass of women on boards can lead to several benefits in terms of board governance, including more robust deliberation, disruption of groupthink, more effective risk management, higher quality monitoring of management, and more systematic work."[14] This is a great place to start. The reality for women who find themselves as the "only" woman at the table or on the stage is a feeling of isolation. Where there is low representation, then the risks of stigmatization and tokenism increase.

The 30 percent minimum can shift the culture of a leadership team quickly. Often we assume it's better to make small, incremental changes (i.e., we will "try out" one woman leader and see what happens). The results are often tokenism and marginalization for the "only" woman at the table. Many of the only's don't last in leadership as a result. If we are going to implement a real cultural shift, we need to do it in a way that will bring transformational gains.

According to the Washington Center for Equitable Growth, "A variety of studies show that establishing a 'critical mass' of at least 30-percent women in corporate leadership enhances firm innovation and overall performance. This is consistent with behavioral research that gender integration improves teams' 'collective intelligence.' In the financial sector in particular, occupational integration decreases systemic risk driven by masculine-stereotyped behaviors encouraged in sex-segregated environments."[15]

Far from being too difficult, it is possible to move toward equity with a simple but intentional posture of listening, learning, and living differently. This can shift our existing cultures and make a way for mutual thriving as women and men learn to lead together.

Things to Think About

- Have a look at your leadership teams. Do they reflect your desire for gender equity?

- Have you listened to people who might be able to help you determine where the barriers are?
- What voices are you not listening to that might be helpful to seek out?
- What have you learned about diversity that might be helpful to you so far?
- How can you implement some changes right now?
- Could you aim for 30 percent women leaders/ representation on your leadership teams?
- What would you need to change/do/implement to achieve that?

THIRTEEN

Never, Ever Give Up

The biggest predictor of success is not IQ, it's resilience.

—ELLEN DUFFIELD

'****ve lived in a few different countries with my family and participated in a "transition training." The transition bridge experience is a tool used by a missionary agency when missionary kids return home from serving in a different culture.[1] The bridge was definitely a family highlight. We did it together. In our setting we used chairs as a bridge. My eight-year-old son was the volunteer and hopped on the first chair in the makeshift bridge. It was solid and straightforward and represented the place he considered his last home—that stage is called "settled." He was asked about how he felt in that place, and he described how much he enjoyed living there and a bit about what it was like. He was invited to take a step to the next chair. It was called "unsettled." It seemed straightforward but under one of the legs of this chair there was a block. It made the chair shaky and unsteady, and my son had to reach out and hang on. This represented the time when he learned he was leaving his home. He was asked to describe how he felt when he found out he was moving to another country, another place, another culture. He said he didn't really know how to feel. He was kind of excited but also afraid. It was unsettling.

This is exactly how this stage in transition works. Something has shifted, changed. You aren't as sure of your footing. You often need to hang on and pay attention to why you are feeling a little unsure and unsettled. The next stage of transition is to the very middle of the transition bridge. It is the chaos stage of transition. In our "chair bridge"-styled enactment it was represented by a large bouncy exercise ball wrapped in plastic. My son took one look and realized quickly that if he tried to step onto it, he would crash and burn. "What will you do?" asked the facilitator. My son looked up at our family watching and whispered the words, "Help me?" Before he even got the words out, my eldest son was by his side, holding the weight of his body and helping him balance on the completely unstable ball representing the chaos of transition. It was such a powerful moment.

Everyone watching could relate to the stage of transition when you haven't quite arrived at the new place but you have let go of the old one. It feels like chaos. Everyone has these moments. We leave the old behind and launch into the new, even before we are steady or feel ready. We could even call this the "faith" zone, where we are required to leap before we fully understand.

The facilitators of the exercise told me that sometimes when they do the bridge with whole families, they tie them together—one parent at the head of the line and one bringing up the rear. When they get to the chaos part of the bridge, they often ask the one in front, "How's your spouse?" Of course they have no idea. They are applying all of their energy just keeping themselves and the kids they are tied to from wiping out. Teams ready to transition into new territory will be going through this together. It'd be wise to pay attention and help each other along.

The step out of chaos for our son led him to another unsteady chair. He could manage it, but it wasn't comfortable yet. I thought this was a very strategic stage. We so long for the comforting conclusion of our transition. We can tire easily, especially after the chaos of letting go of what was familiar. But before the settled feeling in the final stage comes another unsettling one. I think this represents the time you arrive at a new destination but it is still unfamiliar. It may be a house, but it's not your home. You don't feel settled yet because you are in the middle of transition. What you are doing is good but it's still unfamiliar to you.

The facilitator told us this can be a very dangerous place. The expectations are for instant transition, but the realities are much more complex than that. Transitions take time. A few more steps and my son found his solid ground, fully planting himself on the final chair in the "settled" stage and breathing a deep sigh of relief. The rewarding place of transition is what change feels like when it's done. But so often we expect change to be instant and comfortable. This exercise might be helpful as we consider the long work of transition.

Transition Bridge

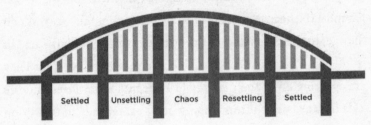

Settled   Unsettling   Chaos   Resettling   Settled

Your venture into the transition of men and women working together might feel unfamiliar and unsettling. Expect it and talk about this with your teams. One of the most powerful and obvious parts of the experience is that no one can transition alone without crashing and burning in the middle. Talk to each other. Take care of each other. Ask for help as you navigate your way. Another takeaway of the encounter was that everyone transitions at different paces. Some people spend a long time feeling the chaos, others jump over it in a day. Allow everyone to take the time they need. Transition takes time. Give yourself that.

One of the most powerful parts of the experience for me was watching my eldest son instinctively help his younger brother. It was tender, natural, and beautiful to behold as a parent. My eldest son is seven years older than his brother, so he is significantly bigger, stronger, and more experienced at transition. We need these kinds of gestures for everyone going through transition. We need people who have been there before to help us navigate. Look for experienced leadership teams who have done the transition to gender equity before. Ask them for guidance and help. Find seasoned and experienced leaders for the transition women need to make toward empowerment. Most important, do it together. Keep track of each other. Check in. Talk it through. Let the instinctive sibling spirit naturally help ease the process.

And give each other time.

Harriet Tubman spent twenty-nine years in slavery. Once free, she spent the rest of her life helping slaves escape. Nelson Mandela spent twenty-seven years in prison before becoming the leader of South Africa. Rosa Parks was forty-two years old when she refused her seat and spent the rest of her life fighting for freedom and equality. Moses spent forty years in the desert before God called him and then spent another lifetime working for freedom. Dietrich Bonhoeffer started fighting Nazism in Germany in 1933 for twelve years until he was killed in 1945.

Change takes time. And those who really change things will keep moving. Keep fighting. Keep pushing against injustice, and keep inviting the future into today.

Stretch Collaboration

As noted earlier, Adam Kahane is an expert in getting people who don't trust each other to collaborate on making a better future. He challenges the notion of traditional negotiation strategies for change. Traditionally people have thought everyone has to agree on the problem and a solution in order to work together. But Kahane has found some deeper truth. You can have people around the table with absolutely different ideas of the problem and different ideas of the solution. But the thing they can agree on is paramount. It's time to change. We want to move. We want to move this situation to a better one.

Instead of long, laborious, time-killing sessions trying to get people to agree on what the problem is or whose fault it is or what the best solutions are, he employs a strategy he calls "stretch collaboration." If you hope to transition your team to a new future, these three stretches to achieve collaboration might be helpful to keep in mind.[2]

Embrace conflict and connection. Engage and assert. Engaging is the listening strategy—leaning into the tension, the conflict. Don't be afraid of confrontation. Don't ignore the problem. Look for the opportunity in the chaos. Listen well and often. As you identify areas that need to change, you must also insist on a change. It can't be all connection (love/listening/relationship) without conflict (power/advocacy/change). Adam said he has mistaken both of these strategies as separate, sometimes thinking that if only people could know and respect each other, things would change. He realized that people do need to know and respect each other (love/proximity/relationship), but that won't necessarily change things. There also has to be conflict. Genuine confrontation and advocacy. Without conflict, there is no change. Embracing and employing them both are strategic ways to keep advancing.

Experiment with the way forward. Co-creation. "The discipline required to discover a way forward creatively is to try something out, step back and look at the result, and then change it, iterating over and over. . . . We need to be present to what is actually happening rather than what we wish would happen," Kahane said. This is very important for gender equity because each situation is unique to local contexts. We can try methods that have worked with others, but they need to be adapted to bear fruit. I found the imagery of the creation account in this stretch interesting. God invited humanity to cocreate together. Resisting "men" fixing the problem or "women" dominating the discussion, the invitation in this stretch is to navigate the way together, just like we were created to do. Consider the example of gardening: we can create some of the conditions for a collective effort to flourish, but we cannot direct it to do so. To try something, adapt it, and then try it again is not failure; it's strategy. Instead of an organizational-chart approach to change, think more like Picasso and create something beautiful. Kahane, quoting Jeff Barnum, said, "The creative process is a process of finding, not of projecting something already seen and known in one's mind." Discover the potential of a shared future together.

Step into the game. Get something done. "If we want to get important things done in complex situations, then we can't spend our time just watching and blaming and cajoling others. We have to step in." Resisting the tendency to blame others will help. One great way to resist blaming is through contributing. Taking personal responsibility for finding solutions will help you own the problem instead of just critiquing it as an observer. Everyone knows it's a lot easier to receive correction from someone who has a stake in the game! As the joke goes, in a ham omelet, the chicken is involved but the pig is committed. No change will happen without the full commitment of everyone involved to step into the game.

Strategic Stages

If you've ever considered yourself a patient person, just get in line behind someone who is slow moving. In a traffic jam or the grocery store checkout, this reality remains a consistent revelation of how much patience I lack! If you are anything like me, you'd like everything to change yesterday.

Some of the most effective strategic stages for long-term change don't happen overnight; they require time. Our impatience at a slow and steady pace will undermine our efforts to change the "muscle memory" of our communities and organizations. The idea of muscle memory is the default mode of our cultures. In other words, you can build beautiful new diverse and creative things, but if you don't change the ideology and processes behind them, they will revert right back to what is most familiar.

How we make these long-term strategic changes in our systems, structures, and relationships must be multifaceted to be successful. The top five strategic stages for managing change over the long haul are giving yourself time, giving yourself permission to fail and learn, creating manageable benchmarks for change, conducting regular evaluations to measure progress, and celebrating forward momentum. Bill Gates reminded us, "We always overestimate the change that will occur in the next two years and underestimate the change that will occur in the next ten. Don't let yourself be lulled into inaction."[3]

McKinsey & Company reported the reason transition toward gender equity has been slow: "Major transformation efforts require steady, broad-based interventions over time. After an initial commitment from the top, significant changes can typically take as many as eight or more years, requiring the close and visible monitoring of progress by the executive team. It's never easy and it's rarely quick."[4]

When I was considering ways to fight human trafficking, I took a long look at the history of fighting the transatlantic slave trade. Any study of an injustice that needs to be confronted and changed will conclude similarly. It will take exposure, intention, direct action, and radical change over a long period of time. Time is possibly the hardest part to accept in our current culture. We like quick and sweeping change. We are addicted to what I call "the Disney myth." We like to imagine a fairy-godmother solution with magical power offering instant transformation! This myth makes us naive about the reality needed to secure real change.

Morgan Stanley declared in their manifesto *The Gender Advantage* a dedication to diversity, because research has proven that it will benefit their business and their customer base and help the world become a better place. But they insist it's not just a declaration; it's an objective. "Achieving gender balance is a long-term objective that also requires progress on issues that have disproportionately affected women and girls, such as sex trafficking, affordable childcare, and maternal healthcare."[5]

If we hope to make the kind of changes necessary for men and women to thrive together, we must dedicate ourselves to long-term objectives with measurable goals. I know it doesn't sound slick or fast, but for those of us who want real change, it is what's required for true transformation.

Jon Acuff wrote a whole book called *Finish* because he was amazed at how many people quit projects before they finish. Ninety-two percent of New Year's resolutions fail. Jon went on a search to uncover the tools to help people cross the finish line. I recommend the book, but let me reiterate three simple things he said are "dials" you can adjust to keep you progressing instead of quitting: set the goal (be clear), create the timeline (measurable goals to monitor your progress), and list the action steps.[6] Much simpler to write than to implement, but all of these are essential.

I was sitting around a table in Cape Town recently, listening to leaders from all different backgrounds and networks sharing their hopes for their country. It was infectious. As they began to share their thoughts, I felt hope for change and possibilities rising in me. As the host of the gathering shared her hope for a reconciled South Africa, she also pointed out that the meal we were having together would have been impossible only twenty-five years ago. I had been part of passionate conversations about the hard and slow work of change. The weariness of trying to live out a dream over a long period of time was showing in the lives of these leaders working for change. Is it really possible to take a dream of reconciliation and make it happen in real life? The answer is a resounding yes! But it will take time and effort. To live out a massive social change will require the commitment of dreamers to dig deep to find hope and keep it alive. Hope is an eternal currency for change, and there is nothing more essential in creating resilience for long-term transformation!

Things to Think About

- Is your vision of equity long-term?
- What might you need to prepare for the long journey of gender equity in your setting?
- If you could pick a chair you were in on this transition, what stage would you be at? How can you move to the next one?
- Are you committed to going the distance?
- Have you set a long-term goal (50 percent women and men leading), and do you have measurable goals to achieve that (in one year we'll be at 30 percent)?

FOURTEEN

Keeping Hope Alive

To live without hope is to cease to live.

—FYODOR DOSTOEVSKY

The enemies of dreams are not always scary monsters. Sometimes the participants look and act rather normal. Most of us don't live in nightmare scenarios; we live in what we would suggest are average ones. And that's partly the problem. When oppression gets familiar, it normalizes itself into our everyday life. Soon we begin to expect certain behaviors and attitudes. We gradually forget what it's like to live a different way. And before we know it, we can't even imagine things being different. We lack the ability to dream of a transformed future. That's how oppression works. It restricts your dreaming ability and destroys your appetite for possibility. If you pay attention to the way we talk about relationships between men and women right now, you will spot the enemies of cynicism and despair—the tools of oppression. They have prevented our capacity to imagine what it would be like to live in a world where women and men flourish together.

I've been invited to speak at some denominational gatherings recently where it has been fascinating to watch them unknowingly uncover behaviors that don't match their beliefs. At least two of them were denominations founded by a woman. Their story had been created featuring strong female leadership, preaching, teaching, and powerful demonstrations of God's favor. But as they looked around their systems and structures, they discovered there were only a few women currently in leadership roles. When they were looking for strong and amazing women communicators, they could think of very few within their own community. How could that be? How could whole denominations, especially those that were launched by women, where women led and spoke, fifty years later have hardly any women leading, few women speaking, and even fewer women launching new initiatives?

Male domination is like gravity. We don't intentionally head in that direction. There is a weight to it. Think about it in the natural: because of gravity we don't have to try to stay planted on the earth even though the earth is currently rushing through space, rotating at a decent speed. Gravity is working all the time. We don't even think about gravity and the implications if it weren't there. We just keep walking around on a rotating, speeding planet in space. Our feet just keep sticking to the earth. The undercurrent of inequity is just like that. Like gravity. If we aren't consciously moving *against* the flow, we are moving with it. Whether we intend to or not.

The whole thing reminds me of going for a swim in Hawaii. I went for a beautiful, refreshing swim on a blazing hot day under the aloha skies of that majestic paradise. I'm a solid swimmer, so I loved diving under the waves and floating in the sea. It was so relaxing and refreshing at the same time. Then it was time to head back in. I looked at the shore but didn't recognize anyone. Actually, I didn't even recognize the shore. It was a little frightening. It turned out that as I was having fun in a refreshing swim, the undercurrent had taken me about a mile away from where I started. And I did not even notice it. Not until I looked up and saw the shore.

Gender inequity is a lot like an undercurrent in our world. We don't have to participate in it; we just have to let it go unchecked and unnoticed. We just have to "float" along with a dominant culture.

Of course, once I figured out what had happened, I immediately began a very hard and long swim, against the current, to get back to my family waiting on the shore. And that is what imagining a better world entails. It entails waking up to the reality of how far we have drifted from the place we want to be.

Looking Forward with Hope

Believing that change is possible is an active work. It is work to refuse the despairing idea that something is impossible. *To believe* is to challenge the status quo and confront the hopeless nature of inequality and injustice. Believing for the future to change is an active confrontation of fear.

How do we fight against this pull toward gender inequity?

We spot the oppression. We *notice* it. The invisibility of this sort of oppression is one of the most dangerous of the times. Every time we shrug and move on, every time we use stereotypes and exercise fear, every time we clam up and refuse to speak up about an injustice, every time we segregate for our own protection, every time we succumb to excusing behaviors (our own included) because of gender, we are slowly participating in the oppression at work on our minds.

One of the ways you can spot oppression in your own life is in your thoughts. *If you cannot imagine the possibility of things changing, it is a sign that you are oppressed.* The Russian philosopher and author Dostoevsky said that when people lose their hope and purpose, they slowly become monsters.[1] Cynicism works its way into our lives through our minds. It changes our thought processes and shrinks our capacity to dream.

In the movie *The Great Debaters*, Denzel Washington, who played the leader of an African American debating club, explains the process. In one of the first meetings he has with the club, he describes in detail the things that Willie Lynch did to slaves. Willie was a hired tool of slave owners who would come to terrorize slaves in order to keep them in line. He would diabolically torture one man and then beat the other men within an inch of their lives. He would not kill them. The slave owners needed their bodies. But Willie took their minds. They were psychologically scarred into submission. They were unable to even imagine escape. Oppression now owned their thoughts. They would not fight back, nor would they leave, because oppression had taken their minds. The teacher in the movie declares that an educator's role is to help students take back their *righteous* minds.[2] I love that.

Many women have lived through torturous moments at the hands of male abusers. Many men have lived belittled and dismissed. Many mothers have smothered, and fathers have ignored, their children. Many male-dominated workspaces have prevented and blocked women with talent, and many women have remained silent for far too long. All of us are weary of cycles of behavior and entrenched attitudes and treatments that have left us scarred with oppressed minds.

Paul, an early dynamic leader in the Jesus movement, suggested we could be "transformed by the renewing of [our minds]" (Romans 12:2). We cannot will ourselves into believing something if we don't believe it. We need to ask for help. We can ask God to renew our collective mind. To give us back our righteous minds. To be transformed. It's time to refuse cynicism and despair in our lives. It's time to turn the spotlight of possibility and hope on the sinister presence of oppression lurking in the back of our minds and in that uneasy feeling in our gut whenever we bring up gender-related injustices. This is the work of imagining a better future.

This is the tradition of the Christian faith. There is a radical prayer in the letter to the Ephesians that we would be able to imagine the possibilities of God's love. Praying for the eyes of our hearts to be enlightened, Paul believed God would show us the possibilities of things we could not even imagine (Ephesians 1:18). He knew God would blow our minds with the possibilities of hope and a future.

The apostle John was stuck imprisoned on the island of Patmos. While there he wrote Revelation, considered to be one of the strangest and most difficult-to-understand books in the Bible. I've got a hunch that the reason it's so hard to understand is that it's beyond human comprehension. We don't think our way into new living; we live our way into new thinking.

John opened the book with a vision of Jesus as the risen, conquering King. Jesus is beyond any description and is embedded with absolute authority. As René Breuel put it in his exposition of Revelation, "The picture John paints of Jesus in charge is one that ensures every dictator knows he has an expiration date."[3] Much of the book is a description of the power and the glory and the strength and the worthiness of Jesus. John painted a portrait of Jesus as King of kings, with rulers bowing at his feet and heavenly angels doing his bidding.

The reason John was painting this picture of Jesus as the ultimate authority was to help the Christians of his day deal with the numbing and fear-inducing cynicism of the Roman oppression they were living under. He needed them to know (comprehend/imagine) another reality. He needed them to dream about a different possibility. He wanted them to reimagine their lives in the context of God's kingdom. They were not just spokes stuck in a wheel that inevitably turns toward injustice. They were disruptive agents, launched to stop the wheel of injustice from turning at all. They were lights in a dark and corrupted generation. They were a city on a hill. The salt of the earth. They were examples, witnesses, worshipers of the God who will reconcile all things, heal all people, and bring peace on earth as it is in heaven.

He was helping them to reimagine a different future. A future that ends with healing for the nations. In *The Prophetic Imagination*, Walter Brueggemann suggested that a prophetic imagination is the calling of the church. To help the world re-imagine what could be. To imagine the possibilities.

Can you imagine a world of equality? Can you picture a world where people are no longer limited or judged by their gender? Can you imagine a world where little girls and boys grow up as allies? Can you imagine a world where men and women aren't afraid of each other? Can you imagine us flourishing as we work together?

Imagining a new future looks like losing the fear of what we cannot control and working toward what we can do right now. It's time to lose the old baggage of scarcity that suggests if women make it, fewer men can. It's not a competition. Far from it! A celebration of our strengths will enable all of us to go faster and farther toward making a better world now.

A Celebration of Strengths

Together, let's imagine a world where we celebrate strengths. Women and men side-by-side in boardrooms using their indi-vidual perspectives and experiences to shape strategies that reimagine neighborhoods. Men and women on stages using their unique voices and experiences to inspire people to aim higher, to connect with God. Women and men using their giftedness to lead children to become the best version of themselves instead of the cookie-cutter varieties offered them by mainstream culture.

This is not just an exercise for our heads. It's not simply a vision exercise. This is deeply spiritual work because choosing to see the possibilities of a world without sexism is a God-breathed activity. It has the capacity to release hope into the "too hard" of this issue. It has the objective to motivate us to try to apply what we see.

Like all amazing athletes who use visioning as a driver for excellence, this kind of prophetic imagining will drive us to a future that is coming and will not let us be satisfied with less than God's plan. And to be sure, your imagination will be necessary for you to see it. This world does not have many amazing examples of a strength-based mutual flourishing of women and men being better together. The news is dominated by the opposite, and our reactions to that news will be an important way to direct the future.

So what if we can't do this?

If we can't imagine a world where it's possible for men and women to flourish, then we will revert in a sort of practical, best-case scenario of survival. We will put up barriers to protect ourselves from our own fears. We will shrink back to things that might have worked in the past, even though they are outdated and unable to stand the cultural moment. We cannot allow fear to limit our ability to imagine a better world.

If ever we needed to shine the light of hope and possibility in today's world, it's now. We want to shout the good news of reconciliation! Jesus himself is reconciling all things to God. The relationship between men and women is at the heart of this healing work. This could be the best way to show the world what the power of God can actually do. God can and will liberate us from

brokenness, fear, abuse, biases, prejudices, systems, and structures that limit us instead of release us. God can and will create
leaders who serve each other and the deep needs of the world;
women and men who love, relationships that flourish through
mutuality and equity, and so much more.

Can you imagine being that kind of light to the world right
now? I hope you can. If you can't, then stop and ask God, who is
able to do immeasurably more than we could ever ask or imagine,
to ignite your imagination with the dreams of his kingdom come.

Hope

Nelson Mandela said, "Our human compassion binds us the one
to the other—not in pity or patronisingly, but as human beings
who have learnt how to turn our common suffering into hope
for the future."[4]

Hope is the one ingredient that can transform a crisis into an
opportunity. Hope always starts with the future, and the future
is full of hope. A friend gave me great advice many years ago
when she told me, "Always start the way you want to finish."
In this book I've tried to give you a full look at the possibilities and opportunities for women and men to work together.
Yet without hope, it won't work. It is paramount that we look at
this issue through the lens of hope. This work *is* possible. Hope
defies cynicism, confronts defeatism, and refuses to ignore the
inevitable work required to make the world better. Hope infuses
the impossible with possibility. It encourages and lifts; it calls

people to a greater vision than what is possible on their own. Hope is a driver of energy and resources.

Hope is also a weapon. It's always the weapon of choice for those who believe that history moves toward redemption. I do not mean naivety. This is not pie-in-the-sky, wishful thinking. This hope is staking our actions on our beliefs. It's rooting and establishing ourselves into the soil of God's kingdom. It will require everything we have and much more. It will require God to help us. And what will God give us as a resource that will never run out? Hope. Hope is eternal. In today's cynical and despairing world, and in this particular topic, which leaves the best of us shaking our heads in discouragement at times, this is the secret sauce. Hope is an eternal agency. Hope will last forever (right beside love and faith). Hope is the way we fuel our work of love and the place we put our faith. Hope.

Instilling a sense of hope is not some basic idea to motivate people in a Sunday service or a boardroom office but leave them desperate in everyday life. And we certainly can't afford to offer anyone false hope. We recognize false hope by its crummy quality and lack of strategy. A sign you aren't offering real hope is when people roll their eyes when you announce change. Real hope is a conduit of change. It's the wide-eyed optimist who brings a strategy to the table. It's the leader who not only announces the need but demonstrates the audacity to set measurable goals. It's the joy-infused dreaming of a team demonstrated by their dogged, determined efforts toward changing the present. Using hope is the most important strategic advance when it comes to women and men working together.

So I'm ending this book how I hope I started—with hope. I've had way too many conversations with both male and female leaders about this issue that are cynical (nothing will change anyway), defeatist (we can't win, so we won't even bother playing), or escapist (not our problem). Those conversations are the sound of despair. But I've also heard a different sound. Women speaking, men dreaming, leaders listening, people apologizing, parents believing, and many folks cheering. The possibility of living the future now fills me with hope. And I'm praying that this hope looks determined (it's hard but it's worth it), unified (we can do it together), and committed (let's give it a shot). I pray that some of the ideas and strategies in this book might compel you to action, but even deeper than that I pray that you would be filled with hope. The future is filled with possibilities, and I'm believing that we might be the ones to see them come alive, together. Women and men thriving is one of those dreams. We desperately need one another in this difficult world.

The vision of mutual flourishing doesn't end with unity of the genders. Restored relationships are how the greater vision of transformation for the whole world is possible. The end goal is *always* about creating a better world. It's about humanity's ultimate job to reconcile *all* things to God. The unity of the genders—the mutual flourishing of men and women doing that together—is a main way that the ultimate job will get done. That's why hope is relentless in this regard. We will need hope to get us started on equity and partnership, but we will also need hope to use our partnerships for something much bigger than us. The reconciliation of men and women is both a sign to this world that it's possible to change the future, and it's an agency of that change. Think about it. Men and women are connected at every conceivable level. From birth to death. There is no way to completely sever the relationship between us. Which means that instead of despairing the inevitable cost of it, we should be able to celebrate the possibilities of it. That's hope.

Let that hope infuse you with the ability to drag the future promise of mutual flourishing into the present reality of inequality. Let it help you cling to the cross and begin the journey of transforming your mind, your actions, and the fruit that your life will bear. Let that hope be the fuel that keeps driving you on the long walk to live out the freedom that God has for men and women together. Let that hope help you in healing relationships so we can start living a new future today.

Things to Think About

- Start imagining what equity would look like in your life. Write out a vision for your life. Imagine everyone in your family and community thriving in a mutually flourishing relationship. What does it look like? Take some time to really imagine what that could be. Ask God to keep enlarging your capacity for imagination.
- Are there men and women in your influence who need releasing from bondages of cultural expectations or fear or systems? Pray for them.
- Imagine Jesus entering your world (home, office,

church). What would he say? What would he do? Who would he heal? Who would he invite to the decision tables? Whose feet would he wash? What tables would he turn over?

- Get together a team of people to imagine out loud together. Sketch out the dream.

Acknowledgments

've heard it takes a village to raise a child, but I had no idea how many people it would take to make this book. I'm convinced that this subject is a timely look at some deeply important truths, and part of the reason I'm sure of this is because it was hard to do. One thing I've figured out living this life is the harder the resistance, the more important the task! This book had an internal resistance to it, a difficulty that could only be understood in light of the pressure against its message. I am deeply aware of all the women in the world who are still fighting for basic human rights. Women whose voices are strong and capable and better than mine but remain unheard and buried under oppression. I'm hoping this work might lighten that weight. To all the men who are tired of spectating and shrugging in the midst of this situation, your commitment to make a change is a hopeful sign on the horizon of the future. Thank you. Thanks to my husband, Stephen, for partnering in this kingdom work. My boys, Zion,

Judah, and Moses, are warriors who wield weapons of hope and grace and goodness; they are a nonstop source of encouragement to me and a sign that this world is destined to get better.

I am deeply grateful to a whole host of people who helped make this happen. Thanks to Alex Field, book agent extraordinaire, and the W Publishing Group at HarperCollins Christian Publishing for pursuing this project. Debbie Wickwire, the editor of champions, who instead of just sending my original mess of thoughts back to me, took a deep breath, dug in, and went to work. Thank you from the bottom of my heart. Your effort lent me the strength and wisdom I so desperately needed. The Global Leadership Network asked me to speak on an extremely sensitive and difficult topic in the middle of a turbulent time. Their bravery to stand for truth (when running for cover would have been easier) is a great example of leadership, and I'm so proud to stand with you. Tom De Vries and team, this book wouldn't have happened without your invitation. Brandon Laird, your support and abilities made this work better! Also, World Relief, thanks for doing your transformational work and letting me tell folks about it!

Lisa Jernigan, the Amplify Peace journey is a nonstop firehose of transformational life experiences. I'm so grateful we get to share those. Making peace is an adventure with you—I'm so honored to be involved. Also, Cal, thanks for being such a good man—cheering, supporting, and encouraging this adventure! Autumn Katz, I'm not even sure we understood how significant our collaborating would become! Your vision and excellence have enabled me to do things I love. Thank you and look out future—I'm calling you the dream-maker, 'cause that's what you are. The team of mighty women who lead the Brave Global movement are incredible examples of how empowerment looks in real life. All of them inspire me; they stand knee-deep fighting oppression but also remain full of hope and have enormous space for dreaming and living justice in real life. Noemi Chavez, Miley Waterman, Lisa Barnes, and Priscilla Santos—you inspire and encourage me. I'm so grateful for your example and influence in my life and this world! Kerry Chevreau, my executive assistant, Canadian Brave Global fire-starter, friend, and such good company. Thanks for your every effort to make my life manageable and moving forward—you are such a gift!

Last year when I hosted the first women speakers' boot camp (a two-day workshop for aspiring women speakers), I was floored when I looked around the room. There to support, volunteer, and be available with whatever they could do to help was a host of mighty women: Tammy Dunahoo, Deb Walkemeyer, Lisa Smith, Lori Herman, Christy Wimber, to name a few powerhouses who lent their gifts, vision, experiences, and resources. It's hard to explain how your presence and servant-heartedness filled me with hope for a different future—thank you, friends.

Speaking of friends, Janet Munn, your wisdom, advice, prayers, encouragement, example, and academic prowess have been a constant source of fuel for my fire. Thank you. Pauline, Barb, Stacy, Kristine, Kerri, Taanis, and Amy, my "sacred friends," thanks for listening, loving, and praying. Experiencing God's grace together is a wild and holy thing. The Boundless Prayer team (you know who you are)—let's keep "wasting" our time on

God! Bob Goff has been hope, healing, and help to me on this journey of discovering how to set my dreams afloat. No wonder he's an expert with balloons. Also, I have a yellow bike, a beach cruiser named Freedom, that I ride with a big fat smile because Bob gave it to me. The bike is awesome, but the freedom is even better than I thought. Alan and Deb Hirsch, legends and friends. Alan, every tear matters. Reggie Joiner, Andy Stanley, Carey and Toni Nieuwhof, Eugene Cho, Dave Ferguson, Anthony Delaney, Bruxy Cavey, Steve Carter, Brad Lomenick, Tyler Reagan, Aaron White, Mike Frost, Hugh Halter, and the host of men who have refused to stand by and watch, who have stepped up and made room. Thank you. Your support has made us all better together. I'm thrilled to live this out with you. Here's to a better world for our children.

Notes

Chapter 1: Starting from the Future

1. Danielle Strickland, *The Liberating Truth: How Jesus Empowers Women* (Oxford, England: Lion Hudson, 2011).
2. "How Empowering Girls and Women Can Change the World," Plan International Canada, accessed June 3, 2019, https://stories .plancanada.ca/how-empowering-girls-and-women-can-change -the-world/.
3. "The 1 in 6 Statistic," 1in6.org, accessed June 3, 2019, https://1in6 .org/get-information/the-1-in-6-statistic/.
4. Liz Plank, "Most Perpetrators of Sexual Violence Are Men, So Why Do We Call It a Women's Issue?," Divided States of Women, November 2, 2017, https://www.dividedstatesofwomen.com/2017 /11/2/16597768/sexual-assault-men-himthough.

Chapter 2: What It Could Look Like and Why It Matters

1. All definitions here are from yourdictionary.com, accessed June 3, 2019, https://www.yourdictionary.com.
2. Curt Rice, "How Blind Auditions Help Orchestras to Eliminate Gender Bias," *Guardian* (international edition), October 14, 2013,

https://www.theguardian.com/women-in-leadership/2013
/oct/14/blind-auditions-orchestras-gender-bias.

3. World Economic Forum, "The Global Gender Gap Report 2017,"
November 2, 2017, http://www3.weforum.org/docs/WEF_GGGR
_2017.pdf.

4. Jonathan Woetzel et al., "How Advancing Women's Equality
Can Add $12 Trillion to Global Growth," McKinsey & Company,
September 2015, https://www.mckinsey.com/featured-insights
/employment-and-growth/how-advancing-womens-equality-can
-add-12-trillion-to-global-growth.

5. Ellen Duffield, "Margaret Alva, Federal Secretary of the All India
Congress Committee, Salzburg Global Seminar," September
2006, in *Brave Women: Building Bridges to Transformation, a
Compendium (BRAVE Leaders)* (Ontario: Shadow River Ink,
2018), 203, quoted in Linda Tarr-Whelan, *Women Lead the Way:
Your Guide to Stepping Up to Leadership and Changing the World*
(San Francisco: Berrett-Koehler Publishers, 2009).

6. Christine Amour-Levar, "Rwanda, A Success Story of Women of
Empowerment," HuffPost, January 5, 2018, https://www
.huffingtonpost.com/entry/rwanda-a-success-story-of-women
-empowerment_us_5a4f1d87e4b0ee59d41c09ad.

7. Laurel Stone, "Can Women Make the World More Peaceful?,"
Guardian (international edition), August 11, 2014, https://www
.theguardian.com/global-development-professionals-network
/2014/aug/11/women-conflict-peace-society.

8. Leymah Gbowee, *Mighty Be Our Powers* (New York: Beast Books,
2013); Leymah Gbowee, *Pray the Devil Back to Hell*, directed by
Gini Reticker (Warren, NJ: Passion River Films, 2009), DVD.

9. Duffield, *Brave Women*, 26.

10. *The Future of Jobs*, Global Challenge Insight Report (Geneva:
World Economic Forum, 2016), http://www3.weforum.org/docs
/WEF_Future_of_Jobs.pdf.

11. Vivian Hunt, Dennis Layton, and Sara Prince, "Why Diversity
Matters," McKinsey & Company, January 2015, https://www

.mckinsey.com/business-functions/organization/our-insights
/why-diversity-matters.

12. "The Case for Gender Parity," *Global Gender Gap Report 2017,*
(Geneva: World Economic Forum, 2017), http://reports.weforum
.org/global-gender-gap-report-2017/the-case-for-gender-parity/.

13. *Global Gender Gap Report 2018,* (Geneva: World Economic
Forum, 2018), http://www3.weforum.org/docs/WEF_GGGR
_2018.pdf.

14. "The World Food Programme Leads the Way in Fighting Hunger
Worldwide," Newstalk, November 27, 2017, https://www.newstalk
.com/news/the-world-food-programme-leads-the-way-infighting
-hunger-worldwide-519386.

15. *WPF Gender Policy 2015–2020* (Rome: World Food Programme,
2015), 4, https://documents.wfp.org/stellent/groups/public
/documents/communications/wfp276754.pdf?_ga=2.238723200
.1281940074.1568133415-619611922.1568133415.

16. Jill Filipovic, "How Gender Equality Is the Friend of the Family,"
Guardian (US edition), April 20, 2012, https://www.theguardian
.com/commentisfree/cifamerica/2012/apr/20/gender-equality
-friend-family.

17. Sandra Pepera, "Why Women in Politics?," Women Deliver,
February 28, 2018, https://womendeliver.org/2018/why-women
-in-politics/.

Chapter 3: The Truth About Oppression

1. Ioana Latu and Marianne Schmid Mast, "The Effects of Stereotypes
of Women's Performance in Male-Dominated Hierarchies:
Stereotype Threat Activation and Reduction Through Role
Models," *Gender and Social Hierarchies: Perspectives from Social
Psychology,* ed. K. Faniko et. al. (Abingdon, UK: Routledge, 2015),
https://www.researchgate.net/publication/282848827_The_effects
_of_stereotypes_of_women's_performance_in_male-dominated
_hierarchies_Stereotype_threat_activation_and_reduction
_through_role_models.

2. Joyce He and Sarah Kaplan, "The Debate About Quotas," website for the Rotman School of Management's Institute for Gender and the Economy, October 26, 2017, https://www.gendereconomy.org/the-debate-about-quotas/.

3. Nicholas D. Kristof and Sheryl WuDunn, *Half the Sky: Turning Oppression into Opportunity for Women Worldwide* (New York: Vintage Books, 2010), xvii.

4. Harry Bruinius, "Churches Struggle with Their #MeToo Moment," *Christian Science Monitor*, April 20, 2018, https://www.csmonitor.com/USA/Politics/2018/0420/Churches-struggle-with-their-MeToo-moment.

5. Allan G. Johnson, "What Can We Do?," *Privilege, Power, and Difference* (New York: McGraw-Hill, 2001), https://www.cabrillo.edu/~lroberts/AlanJohnsonWhatCanWeDO001.pdf.

Chapter 4: A Vision for Reconciliation

1. "The Deeper Magic from Before the Dawn of Time," WikiNarnia, the Chronicles of Narnia Wiki, based on *The Chronicles of Narnia* series by C. S. Lewis, https://narnia.fandom.com/wiki/The_Deeper_Magic_from_Before_the_Dawn_of_Time.

2. See 2 Corinthians 5:18.

Chapter 5: How We Feel

1. Tanya Basu, "How a Paralyzed Man Walked Again," *Time*, September 24, 2015, http://time.com/4042930/paralyzed-man-walks-again/.

2. Jeff Lockyear, Global Leadership Network training presentation, December 2018, interview with author.

3. Seth Richardson, "Is (Healthy) Cross-Gendered Ministry Even Possible?," Missio Alliance, June 14, 2018, https://www.missioalliance.org/is-healthy-cross-gendered-ministry-even-possible/.

4. William Peters and Charlie Cobb, "A Class Divided" (transcript), *Frontline*, aired March 26, 1985, on PBS, https://www.pbs.org/wgbh/pages/frontline/shows/divided/etc/script.html.

5. Peters and Cobb, "A Class Divided."

6. Peters and Cobb, "A Class Divided."

7. Richardson, "Is (Healthy) Cross-Gendered Ministry Even Possible?"

8. Wikipedia s.v. "Ubuntu Philosophy," last modified September 8, 2019, 18:10, https://en.wikipedia.org/wiki/Ubuntu_philosophy.

9. Paul J. H. Schoemaker and Steven Krupp, "6 Principles That Made Nelson Mandela a Renowned Leader," *Fortune*, December 5, 2014, http://fortune.com/2014/12/05/6-principles-that-made-nelson-mandela-a-renowned-leader/.

10. Seth Richardson, "Four Things I Need to Hear from My Sisters in Christ," Missio Alliance, October 11, 2018, https://www.missio alliance.org/four-things-i-need-to-hear-from-my-sisters-in-christ/.

Chapter 6: How We Live

1. Lean In (@leanincommunity), "We're at a pivotal moment," Facebook, February 6, 2018, https://m.facebook.com/story.php?story _fbid=1611209458957359&id=288110884600563.

2. Alex Williams, "Canada's Secret History of Segregation," *NOW*, February 18, 2016, https://nowtoronto.com/news/canada-s-secret -history-of-segregation/.

3. "Her Story" (sermon series), The Meeting House, February 3– March 10, 2019, http://www.themeetinghouse.com/teaching /archives/2019/her-story/.

4. Kim Steven Hunt and Robert Dumville, *Recidivism Among Federal Offenders: A Comprehensive Overview* (Washington, DC: United States Sentencing Commission, 2016), https://www.ussc .gov/sites/default/files/pdf/research-and-publications/research -publications/2016/recidivism_overview.pdf.

5. "Restorative Justice and Recidivism," *Research Summary* 8, no.1, Public Safety Canada, January 2003, https://www.publicsafety.gc .ca/cnt/rsrcs/pblctns/jstc-rcdvs/index-en.aspx.

Chapter 7: How We See

1. Gillian Tan and Katia Porzecanski, "Wall Street Rule for the #MeToo Era: Avoid Women at All Cost," Bloomberg,

December 3, 2018, https://www.bloomberg.com/news/articles
/2018-12-03/a-wall-street-rule-for-the-metoo-era-avoid-women
-at-all-cost.

2. Billy Graham, *Just as I Am* (New York: HarperCollins, 1997), 127–29.

3. Sarah Friedmann, "13 Simple Things Women Couldn't Do 50 Years Ago in the US," Bustle, June 30, 2017, https://www.bustle .com/p/13-simple-things-women-couldnt-do-50-years-ago-in -the-us-66601.

4. Richardson, "Four Things I Need to Hear from My Sisters in Christ."

Chapter 8: How We Think

1. Rosabeth Moss Kanter, *Confidence: How Winning Streaks and Losing Streaks Begin and End* (New York: Three Rivers Press, 2006), 8, quoted in Duffield, *Brave Women*, 39 (see chap. 2, n. 5).

2. Francesca Albano, "World Relief's Church Empowerment Zones: This Changes Everything," World Relief, July 12, 2017, https:// worldrelief.org/blog/world-reliefs-church-empowerment-zones -this-changes-everything.

3. He and Kaplan, "The Debate About Quotas," Gender and the Economy, October 26, 2017, https://www.gendereconomy.org /the-debate-about-quotas/ (see chap. 3, n. 2).

4. Malala Yousafzai and Christina Lamb, *I Am Malala* (London: Weidenfeld & Nicolson, 2013).

5. Ellen Duffield, "The Story," BraveWomen.ca, accessed June 9, 2019, http://bravewomen.ca.

6. Kristen Wendt, "Girls' Self Esteem Peaks at Age Nine," NotEnoughGood.com, August 7, 2012, http://notenoughgood .com/2012/08/girls-self-esteem-peaks-at-age-nine/.

7. "Statistics on Girls and Women's Self Esteem, Pressures & Leadership," Heart of Leadership, https://heartofleadership.org/statistics/.

Chapter 9: How We Connect

1. "Get Statistics," National Sexual Violence Resource Center, accessed June 9, 2019, https://www.nsvrc.org/node/4737.

2. "Get Statistics."

3. "20 Mind-Blowing Stats About the Porn Industry and Its Underage Consumers," Fight the New Drug, May 30, 2019, https://fightthenewdrug.org/10-porn-stats-that-will-blow-your-mind/.

4. "20 Mind-Blowing Stats."

5. "How Porn Changes the Brain," Fight the New Drug, August 23, 2017, https://fightthenewdrug.org/how-porn-changes-the-brain/.

6. Monica Gabriel Marshall, "4 Signs Your Man Is Serious About Quitting Porn," *Verily*, August 30, 2017, https://verilymag.com/2017/08/how-to-quit-porn-how-you-know-your-guy-quit-porn.

7. "The Most Viewed Porn Categories of 2017 Are Pretty Messed Up," Fight the New Drug, January 10, 2018, https://fightthenewdrug.org/pornhub-reports-most-viewed-porn-of-2017/.

Chapter 10: How We Act

1. Allison Goldstein, "Sexual Harassment Statistics: Is the Truth in the Numbers?," Statistics Views, March 15, 2018, https://www.statisticsviews.com/details/feature/10906109/Sexual-Harassment-Statistics-Is-the-Truth-in-the-Numbers.html.

2. Abby Young-Powell, "Red Flags, Rulers and Ropes: Creative Approaches to Teaching Gender Equality," *Guardian* (US edition), January 20, 2017, https://www.theguardian.com/teacher-network/2017/jan/20/schools-teachers-students-gender-feminism.

3. Juwairiah Ahmed, "From Gutenberg to the Internet: A Comparison of the Impact of Gutenberg Printing Press and the Internet as Media Technologies," Prezi, April 9, 2013, https://prezi.com/tzwe8klf3anb/from-gutenberg-to-the-internet-a-comparison-of-the-impact-of-gutenberg-printing-press-and-the-internet-as-media-technologies/.

4. Micha Kaufman, "The Internet Revolution Is the New Industrial Revolution," *Forbes*, October 5, 2012, https://www.forbes.com/sites/michakaufman/2012/10/05/the-internet-revolution-is-the-new-industrial-revolution/#6352788747d5.

5. Carl H. Builder, abstract for "Is It a Transition or a Revolution?,"

Futures 25, no. 2 (March 1993), https://www.sciencedirect.com
/science/article/pii/001632879390161L?via%3Dihub.

6. "Wheels," Domestic Abuse Intervention Programs, http://www
.theduluthmodel.org/wheels/.

7. Lord Acton to Bishop Creighton, 1887, in "Lord Acton Writes
to Bishop Creighton . . .," Online Library of Liberty, accessed
June 6, 2019, https://oll.libertyfund.org/quotes/214.

8. "Napoleon Bonaparte and Jesus Christ," Just Jesus, November 25,
2009, https://justjesus.typepad.com/blog/2009/11/napoleon
-bonaparte-and-jesus-christ.html.

9. Adam Kahane, "An Introduction to Power and Love: A
Theory and Practice of Social Change," *Reos Partners* (blog),
December 9, 2009, https://reospartners.com/an-introduction-to
-power-and-love-a-theory-and-practice-of-social-change/.

10. Martin Luther King Jr., *Strength to Love* (Minneapolis, MN:
Fortress, 2010), x–xi.

11. Adam Kahane, *Collaborating with the Enemy: How to Work with
People You Don't Agree with or Like or Trust* (San Francisco:
Berrett-Koehler Publishers, 2017), 49–68.

12. "Men, Commit to Mentor Women," LeanIn.org, accessed June 9,
2019, https://leanin.org/mentor-her.

Chapter 11: Stopping the Blame Game

1. Audre Lorde, *Sister Outsider: Essays and Speeches* (New York:
Ten Speed Press, 2007), 123.

2. Susan Krauss Whitbourne, "5 Reasons We Play the Blame
Game," *Psychology Today*, September 19, 2015, https://www
.psychologytoday.com/ca/blog/fulfillment-any-age/201509/5
-reasons-we-play-the-blame-game.

3. Danielle Strickland, *The Liberating Truth: How Jesus Empowers
Women* (Oxford: Monarch, 2011).

4. "Is the NIV Gender Neutral?," New International Version
(website), https://www.thenivbible.com/niv-gender-neutral.

Chapter 12: Start Now and with You

1. Janis Joplin, vocalist, "Ball and Chain," by Willie Mae Thornton, recorded at Festival Express, Calgary, July 4, 1970, track 14 on *In Concert*, Columbia Records, 1972.

2. Alexis Krivkovich et al., "Women in the Workplace 2018," McKinsey & Company, October 2018, https://www.mckinsey.com /featured-insights/gender-equality/women-in-the-workplace-2018.

3. Krivkovich et al., "Women in the Workplace 2018."

4. Krivkovich et al., "Women in the Workplace 2018."

5. Jeff Lockyear, Global Leadership Network training presentation, December 2018, interview with author.

6. HSBC Bank Canada, *2017 Employment Equity Narrative Report*, https://www.about.hsbc.ca/-/media/canada/en/careers/2017 -employment-equity-narrative-report-en.pdf.

7. HSBC Bank Canada, *2017 Employment Equity Narrative Report*.

8. Adam Kahane, "The Potential of Talking and the Challenge of Listening," The Systems Thinker, accessed July 19, 2019, https:// thesystemsthinker.com/the-potential-of-talking-and-the -challenge-of-listening/.

9. Charlotte Werner, Sandrine Devillard, and Sandra Sancier-Sultan, "Moving Women to the Top: McKinsey Global Survey Results," McKinsey & Company, October 2010, https://www .mckinsey.com/business-functions/organization/our-insights /moving-women-to-the-top-mckinsey-global-survey-results.

10. Werner et al., "Moving Women to the Top."

11. Lockyear, interview with author.

12. Lockyear, interview with author.

13. Rachel Thomas et. al, *Women in the Workplace 2018*, LeanIn.org and McKinsey & Company, https://womenintheworkplace.com /#pipeline-data.

14. He and Kaplan, "The Debate About Quotas" (see chap. 3, n. 2).

15. Will McGrew, "Gender Segregation at Work: 'Separate but Equal' or 'Inefficient and Unfair,'" Washington Center for Equitable

Growth, August 18, 2016, https://equitablegrowth.org/gender
-segregation-at-work-separate-but-equal-or-inequitable-and
-inefficient/.

Chapter 13: Never, Ever Give Up

1. David Pollock, Interaction International, used with permission, https://interactionintl.org.
2. Kahane, *Collaborating with the Enemy*, 39–99.
3. Bill Gates, *The Road Ahead* (New York: Viking Books, 1995), [PAGE].
4. Dominic Barton, Sandrine Devillard, and Judith Hazelwood, "Gender Equality: Taking Stock of Where We Are," McKinsey & Company, September 2015, https://www.mckinsey.com/business -functions/organization/our-insights/gender-equality-taking -stock-of-where-we-are.
5. *The Gender Advantage: Integrating Gender Diversity into Investment Decisions* (Morgan Stanley, 2016), 2, https://www .morganstanley.com/pub/content/dam/msdotcom/ideas/gender -diversity-toolkit/Gender-Diversity-Investing-Primer.pdf.
6. Jon Acuff, *Finish: Give Yourself the Gift of Done* (New York: Penguin, 2017), 163.

Chapter 14: Keeping Hope Alive

1. Fyodor Dostoevsky, *Notes from a Dead House*, trans. by Richard Pevear (New York: Vintage Classics, 2016).
2. *The Great Debaters*, directed by Denzel Washington, screenplay by Robert Eisele and Suzan-Lori Parks (Chicago: Harpo Films, 2007).
3. René Breuel, Urbana Student Missions Conference, 2018.
4. "Short Message by Mr. N. R. Mandela at the 'Healing and Reconciliation Service—Dedicated to HIV/AIDS Sufferers and for the Healing of Our Land,'" (transcript of speech given in Johannesburg, December 6, 2000), nelsonmandela.org, http://db .nelsonmandela.org/speeches/pub_view.asp?pg=item&ItemID =NMS967&txtstr=Our%20human%20compassion%20binds%20 us%20the%20one%20to%20the%20other.

About the Author

Danielle Strickland is an author, speaker, trainer, and global social justice advocate. Her aggressive compassion has served people firsthand in countries all over the world—from establishing justice departments for the Salvation Army to launching global antitrafficking initiatives to creating new movements to mobilize people toward transformational living. Affectionately called the "ambassador of fun," she is host of *DJStrickland Podcast*; cofounder of Infinitum, Amplify Peace, and Brave Global; and founder of Women Speakers Collective. Danielle is married to Stephen and lives in Toronto, Canada, with their three sons. Learn more at www.DanielleStrickland.com.

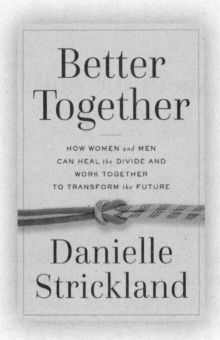